To:

Mr. Pat Welch

My Pal!

Best Wishes!

24-2-2017

The LIFE & DEATH of HOBBY HORSE HALL RACE TRACK

The LIFE & DEATH of HOBBY HORSE HALL RACE TRACK

Documentary on horse racing in The Bahamas
200 years of lost rich Bahamian history.
You never know what you got until you lose it.

Ivan James

Library of Congress Control Number:		2014917849
ISBN:	Hardcover	978-1-4990-6944-0
	Softcover	978-1-4990-6945-7
	eBook	978-1-4990-6943-3

Print information available on the last page.

Rev. date: 02/12/2016

To order additional copies of this book, contact:
Xlibris
1-888-795-4274
www.Xlibris.com
Orders@Xlibris.com
548546

Foreword by

His Excellency Sir Orville Turnquest, GCMG, QC, JP, LLB

I heartily congratulate and commend Mr. Ivan James for the vast research and writing and coordination of this immense work on horse racing in the Bahamas, which not only carefully traces the chronology here of what was known as *the sport of kings* but also offers interesting social commentary on the passing times. I trust that this graphic historical commentary will act as a stimulus leading to the reintroduction of horse racing here.

I have had the privilege of reviewing the book and have happily been able to identify with quite a number of incidences and references that Mr. James cites.

As we move up through the twenty-first century, there is a growing need for us in the Bahamas to commit to published works or to the electronic media details regarding every aspect of life in this country, and that must be done by diligent and enterprising Bahamians, such as Ivan James, who may have a special interest and ability in a particular area.

In that manner, the real history of the real Bahamas will be made available to future generations in order that they may stand proudly upon the shoulders of their forebears and build on their own.

This work by Ivan James, an industrious native of Market Street in Over-the-Hill, Nassau, should be read by every citizen and especially by school children in order that they might know.

Governor-General

2 July 2001

To my loving parents, Carmi Beriah and Mabel James; my son, Ivan James Jr.; and Troy; my siblings, William, Olga, Eric, and C. B. James Jr.; Your Grace Drexel Gomez; Canon William Thompson; Dr. Wavell Thompson; Mr. Winston Saunders, laureate and playwright; Dr. Joseph Evans, urologist; Mr. and Mrs. Tony Allen; Mr. Oscar N. Johnson Sr.; Leroy "Uncle Lee" Archer, mentor; Henry Aleck; Eli Shulman of Chicago; Stan Kurzman and Andie Kurzman of Boston; Mr. Eric Wilmot, journalist; Mr. Gene and Mrs. Roberts Barrett; Mr. and Mrs. Murray Delahay; Mr. and Mrs. Robert Souers; brothers Arnold and Craig Flowers; Tony Sampson; Mr. George and Rita Joblon, New Bedford, Massachusetts, Bruce "Echo" Deveaux; and my *amigo para siempre* (friend for life), former governor-general of the Bahamas Sir Orville Turnquest, who gave me words of encouragement to complete this priceless project. And also, matriarch of the Bahamian Society, Mrs. Lynn Pyfrom Holowesko, former leader of the Senate; and Mrs. Eileen Dupuch Carron, publisher of the *Tribune*. Ms. Thelma Gibson, teacher and character builder, Sir Arlington Butler, Mr. and Mrs. Franklyn Wilson.

Thank you Sir.

Acknowledgments

Writing this book has been a three-year lesson in how history hides in unfamiliar places. The completion of this book is with sadness and joy as several of those who helped create it didn't live to see it in print. Among them was the Honorable Paul A. Adderley, former minister of education and attorney general of the Bahamas. In 1999–2000, Mr. Adderley would spend three to four hours daily at the archives of the Bahamas from Monday to Friday on the research project of Clifton Cay for the Oakes family. I would arrive at the archives just about when Mr. Adderley was about to leave, and after about two weeks, I decided to inform Mr. Adderley on my research project on horse racing in the Bahamas. That information to Mr. Adderley became so fruitful that whenever Mr. Adderley, who had access to the Colonial Office Governors, dispatched files, information on horse racing in the colony was in preponderance, and he would leave that information with the archivist for me. In January 2001, I told Mr. Adderley that I finished my project documentary on horse racing in the Bahamas, and in such a short order, I gave him the manuscript to peruse. After a few days, I went to his law firm to pick up the manuscript. On my arrival, Mr. Adderley wasted no time in extolling my achievement, and he said to me that his daughter, Professor Rozanne Adderley, at Tulane University, Louisiana, USA, is also writing a segment of history, but it didn't look like she was going to finish (smile). Mr. Adderley, thank you, thank you, and I am grateful, for without your help, I would still be in research of the project. Many thanks go to the former director of the Archives of the Bahamas, Dr. Gail Saunders, and her proficient staff who were very helpful and concerned with this project.

Mrs. Lulamae Gray, archivist
Mr. Jolton Johnson, senior archivist
Mrs. Queenie Butler
Mrs. Sherriley Strachan, Ms. Leshelle Delaney
Mrs. Prudence Morris
Mr. David Wood
Former governor-general of the Bahamas Mr. A. D. Hanna, Sir Garet
Finlayson (who still calls me Detry)
Mr. Michael "Learned" Turner, Rene Y. Dean, Mr. Charles "Taxi 871"
Rolle, Mr. "Seeds" Earl Godet
Mr. Elliston Greenslade, commissioner of police
Mr. Maxwell Woodside
Mr. Paul Thompson, former assistant commissioner of police
Mr. and Mrs. Godfrey Fernander
My editor in chief, Asst. Bishop Gilbert A. Thompson, Dr. Philip
Rahming (Fox Hill)
Clergyman Father McSweeney (retired), Arch Deacon Ranfurly
Brown (he still calls me Ivan James "The Shah")
Mr. Bobby "Hammering Hank" Glinton, Mr. Winston Varence
Bishop Simeon Hall, Mr. Boy Wilkinson (they call me "Death"), Mr.
Cass (Mr. Photo), Valerie Barnett
Mr. Malcolm McKay, A. B. Malcolm Foundation
Mr. Sidney French, private collection, Mr. Oswald Isaac's (Mr. President)
Mr. Victor Claridge, private collection, Mr. William Saunders
(Majestic Tours)
Kenneth Seymour (Air Queen), Mrs. Wellington "Britley" Ferguson
Charlie Diamond Kid Gibson, Charlie Pinder Jubilee, Mr. T. "Mighty
Mouse," Fritz "Alteza" Harcourt Bastian, Mr. Percival Munnings,
Cecil Gonzalez, Kenwell "Six" Francis, Basil Nichols
Mr. Vernal Top-of-the-Morning-Sands
Mr. Ralph Williams, Mrs. Remelda Davis (Arawak Cay), Mr. Cyril
Zeke Williams & Mr. Glenn Ride the Man Horse Wilson
Mr. Willie Mays-Francis
Mr. Greg Sir-Harry Woodside
Gary Bain, Boy Pratt "Here," Mr. Roosevelt Godet, Dr. John Godet
(El Spiro), Jockey Eugene Smith Jr.
Alfonzo "Boogalo" Elliott, Pac Buster, Top Executive, Mr. Dake Gonzalez
Bishop Samuel Green, Ms. Angela Cleare,
Ms. Kay Thompson (I Need a Laundry), Mrs. Patrice "Misty" Mortimer,
Mrs. Joycelyn Thompson Bain, Mr. Athama Bowe Historian

Mr. Fred Philips, Oswald Marshall, Mr. George Capron, Mr. Levarity Deveaux

Mr. Wade "411" Wallace and Mr. and Mrs. Patrick Bethell

Mr. Rodney Braynen, Lavoin "Bowe" Stuart, Preston Stuart, Reginald Pratt, Audley Archer Salin "Historian" Smith, Nigel Ingraham, Mr. Roy Glass, Mr. Glenroy Evans, Mr. Eric Cooper, Alonzo Holmes, Leo Woods, Bruce Rolle, Tony Farrington (Mr. Green Sheet)

Peter "Mackey-Dog" Mackey

Carl Armbrister, Mr. Eddie Strachan, John, Big Mike & Donnie Stuart, Mr. Colin "Tony" Bowe

Mr. George Burrows, Ocalastud Farm

Mr. Dudley Lewis, Jockey Anthony "Poker" Huyler, Mr. Lenny "Tropper" Taylor

Ms. Nancy Stands, Mr. Charles (102.9) Carter

Mrs. Esther Barry (The Tribune), Mrs. Maria C. Johnson "My Stenographer"

Stephen Garbo Coakley and Stephen "Daddyo" Mitchell

Mr. Sam "English Sam" Ingraham

Mrs. Abigail Charlow

Mr. Peter Hall

Now the author will give full recognition to the quote by the Bahamas first prime minister, Sir Lynden Oscar Pindling, "Those who don't fight for the Bahamas don't deserve to have it." The following are the surnames of the families of Harbour Island, Spanish Wells, and Eleuthera Island, whose forbears volunteered to join the gallant Colonel Andrew Deveaux expedition to recapture the Bahamas from being a Spanish domain in 1783.

Roberts, Saunders, Braynen, Higgs, Sturrup, Percentie, Curry, Kelly, Petty, Sears, Parks, Pinder, Russell, Sawyer, Sweeting, Bethell, Clarke, Archer, Albury, Pierce, Kemp, Barnett, Cash, Weatherford, Collins, Low, Charlow, Thompson, Sands, Young, Hudson, Kay, Brady Dubois, *our heroes of the Bahamas.*

And finally, after reading the manuscript, the silent philanthropist Mr. Frank Forbes of Sigma Management said this book must be published for the future generations for them to know.

Thank you, thank you.

Ivan Abidial James

"HOBBY HORSE HALL"

The name rolls upon the tongue
And brings a cheerful picture to the mind
The only race track of its kind in the world
You never know what you got until you lose it!

Hobby Horse Hall

The name rolls upon the tongue

And brings a cheerful picture to the mind

The only racetrack of its kind in the world

You never know what you got until you lose it!

The rainbow sign at the entrance of the clubhouse creates a warm reception for the tourists. Through these gates have passed the most important people in the world!

Colonel Andrew Deveaux

(Courtesy of the Senate)

Andrew Deveaux, loyalist officer in the British forces during the American Revolutionary War, was born in South Carolina. Exiled in St. Augustine, Florida, he heard of the sufferings of Nassauvians under the Spanish. With some of his old comrades and a small band of volunteers from Harbour Island and Eleuthera, he daringly recaptured New Providence in 1783.

Deveaux House, Port Howe, Cat Island

(Courtesy of Bahamas Information Services)

Deveaux House, Port Howe, Cat Island, is believed to have been built by Colonel Andrew Deveaux, a loyalist who recaptured New Providence from the Spanish in 1783 and was granted one thousand acres of crown land in Cat Island.

THE DEVEAUX HOUSE, PORT HOWE, CAT ISLAND

The Deveaux House at Port Howe, Cat Island, is believed to have been built by Colonel Andrew Deveaux, a Loyalist, who recaptured New Providence from the Spaniards in 1783. We have evidence that Colonel Deveaux was granted 1,000 acres of land on San Salvador as Cat Island was then called. Moses Deveaux, said to be the son of Colonel Andrew Deveaux occupied the house and his ten children were born there. His grand-daughter, Charlotte Anita Deveaux Bowe lived there in the early part of this century.

The house, according to Mrs. Bowe, originally contained thirteen rooms. Artisans from France helped in its construction and its elaborate plasterwork. There were five rooms upstairs including a living-room, five rooms downstairs and three in the attic. The front of the house faced the sea and the garden was beautifully landscaped. There were wide verandas both upstairs and down. The upstairs veranda was jalousied with wooden shutters and the inside doors were of mahogany.

As was the custom, the kitchen with its fire-place and chimney was built separately, not far from the main house. It is believed that cotton once grew on the plantation and later pineapples were shipped from Port Howe. Sisal was also cultivated there in the early part of this century.

Ivan James Productions

Presents

A Documentary on Horse Racing in
the Bahamas, 1782–1977

Welcome to nostalgia racing from Hobby Horse Hall,
the only racetrack of its kind in the world. You never
know what you got until you lose it!

Horse racing started in the Bahamas over two hundred years ago.
In 1782, Fort Nassau was captured by the Spaniards for the last
time when Don Juan de Cagigal, governor-general of Cuba and the
Havannah, attacked New Providence with five thousand men. The
Spaniards retained nominal possession of the Bahamas until the
conclusion of the war between Spain and Great Britain in 1783.

Before news of peace had crossed the Atlantic in 1783, Andrew
Deveaux, a loyalist colonel of the South Carolina Militia, invaded
New Providence to defeat the Spaniards and regain the islands for
Great Britain. In a dispatch describing this exploit, the gallant colonel
states:

Being in exile in St. Augustine, Florida, at the time, I undertook this expedition at my own expense and embarked my men, which did not exceed sixty-five, and sailed for Harbour Island where I recruited additional men over the next four or five days. From thence, I set sail for my object, which I carried about in daylight with three of their formidable galleys on the fourteenth of April. I immediately summoned the Grand Fortress to surrender, which was about a mile from the fort I had taken. My force never at any time consisted of more than 220 men.

Colonel Deveaux's gallant expedition brought the military history of Fort Nassau to an honorable close. The Spaniards never again returned to attack the islands.

Colonel Andrew Deveaux was born in South Carolina.

Lord Dunmore arrived in the colony in 1787 to become royal governor of the Bahamas. In his findings, Fort Nassau was in disrepair, and His Excellency selected Barnett Hill that overlooked the harbor's western entrance to build the historical Fort Charlotte.

THE
BAHAMA GAZETTE
NULLIUS ADDICTUS JURARE IN VERBA MAGISTRI.

Vol. XII.   From TUESDAY *June* 23, to FRIDAY *June* 26, 1795.   No. 851.

NASSAU, NEW-PROVIDENCE: PRINTED BY JOHN WELLS.

In 1790, 420 acres of Crown land was granted to Colonel Andrew Deveaux. Colonel Deveaux immediately sold the land to Robert Hunt, King's consul to Governor Dunmore, for £450 pounds. One hundred four acres retained by Mr. Hunt, and the remaining 316 acres was returned to the king. That acreage today consists of the Cable Beach Golf Course and Prospect Ridge surrounding properties. The 104 acres became the farm known as Hobby Horse Hall. In 1795, an ad appeared in the *Bahamas Gazette* and read in part:

To Be Leased
For any term, not less than one, or no more than seven years.

> The Farm situated 4 miles west of the town of Nassau known by the name of Hobby Horse Hall, containing 104 acres, forty of which are under good fence. On the premises are a good comfortable dwelling house, an excellent kitchen and a Negro Houser. Apply to John Cunningham.

> Nassau, March 31, 1795.

In 1796, Lord Dunmore was ordered by the king to return to England immediately. It is interesting to note that Hobby Horse Hall Racecourse (one mile) was designed and built by engineering minds simultaneously with the historical Fort Charlotte. In 1921, 126 years later, a writer referred to Hobby Horse Hall as the Dunmore Track. Governor Dunmore assumed the governorship of the Bahamas after serving terms as governor of New York and Virginia. Having an equestrian background, did Governor Dunmore direct his engineering department to design and build Hobby Horse Hall Racecourse out of the King's Treasury for his personal enjoyment?

No record of Hobby Horse Hall Farm being a slave plantation.

Why did Governor Dunmore purchase one thousand lengths of cedar pine ten feet long?

The inside and outside rails of a one-mile oval course is equal to 10,560 feet.

Robert Hunt became commander in chief for a short term until John Forbes was appointed lieutenant governor. November 1796, William Dowdeswell became royal governor of the Bahamas from 1796 to 1801.

In December 1798, another ad appeared in the *Bahamas Gazette* and read in part

To Be Rented
and Entered Immediately

That pleasant sporting seat called Hobby Horse Hall,

> about three miles to the west of Fort Charlotte, on the premises are a neat dwelling house, kitchen and outbuildings which are situated in the center of a racecourse of one mile round, under a cedar fence. A Negro man who is a good house servant, and very well acquainted with the management of horses will be hired with the above premises. Some articles of furniture will also be sold, if wanted by the person

who rents the seat, at a fair appraisement. For terms
and further particulars, apply to Thomas Forbes.

In 1802, Robert Hunt was suspended from the king's consul by the
then governor John Halket (1802–1804).

In 1810, Mr. William Cracknell purchased Hobby Horse Hall
Sporting Seat from a provost marshal sale for two hundred pounds
(£200) from Mrs. Anna Maria Franks, wife of Moses Franks, former
attorney general of the colony from 1790 to 1807. Anna Maria Franks
received presents of title for Hobby Horse Hall Sporting Seat from
her brother, Benjamin Lord, Esq., a most successful merchant in the
town of Nassau.

Hobby Horse Hall Sporting Seat remained active, and another ad
appeared in 1814.

> **Notice.**
>
> The Subscriber begs leave to inform the Public, that he has lately Leased, for a term of years, from the Proprietor, Mr. William Cracknell. All that Tract of Land, known by the name of Hobby Horse Hall, and from the expences attending the same and keeping the grounds in order trusts there will be no objections to his making the following charges, viz.
>
> For every Horse entered to run on the Race Course, one dollar.
>
> For all Carriages visiting the Race Course on the Race Days, at the rate of one shilling per Wheel.
>
> And for Saddle Horses, one shilling.
>
> JOHN WALKER.
>
> Dec. 1 1814

Notice

> The subscriber begs leave to inform the public that
> he has lately leased for a term of years from the
> Proprietor, Mr William Cracknell, all that tract of
> land, known by the name Hobby Horse Hall, and
> from the expenses attending the same and keeping
> the grounds in good order, trusts there will be no
> objections to his making the following charges, viz

>> For every horse entered to run on the
>> racecourse, $1,
>> For all carriages visiting the racecourse on the
>> race days,
>> 1 shilling per wheel, and
>> For saddle horses, 1 shilling.

> John Walker
> December 1, 1814

Match races were basically the theme for horse racing in the colony.

During the years 1818 to 1826, the English Newmarket Handicapping System was implemented.

1826 Nassau Races

> The Nassau subscription plate of $100 will be run for
> all horses.
> Weight for age: five-year-olds, nine stones six pounds,
> four-year-olds, eight stones ten
> pounds, and three-year-olds, seven
> stones six pounds.
> Three pounds extra weight allowed for all horses.
> Heats once around and a distance (one mile and a
> furlong).

Entrance Fee: $5

Gentleman Riders

It is interesting to note that horse racing became the first national sport of the colony of the Bahamas and the United States of America, where slave jockeys like Austin Curtis, Ned and Monkey Simon, rode their way to freedom in the Virginia and North and South Carolina, known as the racehorse region of the United States. In the colony of the Bahamas, only gentleman riders were allowed.

-from the book *The Great Black Jockeys* by Edward Hotaling

Sir James Carmichael Smyth, royal governor 1829–1835

William Colebrooke 1835–1837

Sir Francis Cockburn 1837–1844

George Benvenuto Mathew 1844–1849

Sir George B. Mathew 1844-1849.

Governor George Mathew, with his equestrian background, was very much involved in horse racing in the colony during his tenure as commander in chief. In March 14, 1846, a horse racing bill, Ninth of Victoria, no. 88, chapter 15, was passed in the assembly and read in part that the Queen's Treasury will grant annually one hundred pounds (£100) to the Bahamas Turf Club for colonial purse races to be used as an incentive for the residents of the colony to enhance the breed of racehorses.

The first colonial purse race was run in December 1846. John Pinder's horse, Rodney, won in 1846 and 1847. Governor Mathew owned the racehorse Lapidog. In 1848, His Excellency sent a dispatch to the Bahamas Turf Club declaring December 21, 22, 23, 1848, as the dates for the colonial purse races and some changes for this year's event.

His Excellency stipulated the following:

(1) That no horse shall be entitled to win a colonial purse for more than two successive years.
(2) That not less than three horses shall bona fide contest each race.

The Turf Club members were very disturbed with His Excellency's stipulation, and they acted with protocol and sent a press release to the local newspaper to inform the public on the upcoming colonial purse race dates.

The stewards of the Bahamas Turf Club beg leave to inform the public that His Excellency, The Governor, has declared December 21st, 22nd, 23rd, 1848 the dates for the upcoming Colonel Purse Races.

The Stewards of the Bahamas Turf Club is not in agreement with His Excellency's stipulations and the Governor went contrary to the English Newmarket Rules of Racing and the Act of Assembly.

> John Pinder, G. P. Wood
> Mr. Marriott
> Alva Brook, Sect.
> Mr. Vesey Munnings
> Bahamas Turf Club Members

His Excellency saw this press release to be very disparaging and insulting to the highest office of the land and suspended John Pinder from the Legislative Consul, Mr. Wood from the Port Department, and Mr. Marriott, J. P. License.

A petition was sent to the colonial secretary of state to have the Queen remove Governor Mathew from the colony, and the following charges were made:

(1) The governor is personally attacking Her Majesty's subjects.
(2) The governor is a philanderer, not fit for office of the Queen.
(3) The governor's wife has recently divorced him and claimed adultery.
(4) Affidavit by several people stated that late at night, a Ms. Dorsett was seen entering the governor's compound.

(5)   His Excellency suspended them for a matter irrelevant of the people's business but for being stewards of the Bahamas Turf Club.

December 1848 Colonial Purse Festive Race Entrants:

Rodney	10st. 9 lbs.
Lapidog	10st.
Whitsidon Marc	9st.
Ellen	9st.
Jessie	8st. 2lbs.
Fanney	7st. 12lbs.
Bain's Colt	7st. 6lbs.
Rocket	7st. 3lbs.
Pizarro	7st. 3lbs.
Sally	7st.

All other island-bred horses--a feather--mares and gelding allowed three pounds.

Due to the suspension of the Turf Club stewards, the dates for the colonial purse races were cancelled for December 1848.

His Excellency received a dispatch from the secretary of state in January 1849 informing His Excellency that Her Majesty had not confirmed the suspension of Mr. Wood as executive councilor or Archdeacon Frew and Mr. Pinder as members of the Legislative Council and the restoration of Mr. Marriott to the Commission of the Peace.

With that acknowledgement and the House of Assembly meeting in a day or two, a strange thing happened. Mr. William Doyle tabled a bill to repeal the Ninth of Victoria, no. 88, chapter 15 Racing Bill of 1846 and expressed reasons why. He stated that the Queen's Treasury could not afford to subsidize the Bahamas Turf Club and selective members anymore. Mr. John Pinder debated that a sinister plot was behind the bill and cited the governor was seeking revenge. He said that this bill would create great hardship on the Turf Club members because the operators obtained a loan from the Nassau Bank in the sum of £150 for five years to upgrade the racecourse oval and grandstand, and the debt balance was £100. With due process of the first, second, and third readings, the bill to repeal the Ninth of Victoria Racing Act was passed. Governor George Benvenuto Mathew was relieved of his governorship of the colony, and John Gregory became royal governor of the colony of the Bahamas.

The famous racehorse Lapidog was auctioned at Vendue House. Former Governor Mathew left the Bahamas, and he died in 1854. John Pinder's horse, Rodney, continued his winning ways on the Wednesday, June 14, 1854, match race and won over Mr. Coxworthy's Charlie for fifty (£50) pounds prize money. Another race was run on that day. It was called the footrace, which excited a good deal of merriment. The distance was two furlongs (quarter mile) with four hurdles of three and a half feet high. The footrace was won by a gunner belonging to the royal military and a sergeant and private of the Third West Indian Regiment.

Was the Bahamas the first to implement the hurdles in the West Indies and later used in all international track-and-field events?

His Excellency Sir A. and Lady Bannerman and family were among the numerous assemblages present. The militia band of the Third West Indian Regiment was stationed under a tent and played at intervals, thus contributing greatly to the hilarity of the scene.

In 1863, a journalist wrote about the racing frenzy of the Bahamian people. The cultural sporting events were horse racing, football, rugby, and cricket. No Junkanoo!

1863 Nassau Cup Race

Nassau Guardian
Special Correspondent

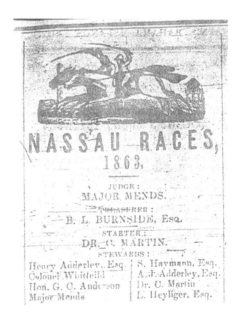

It was a long time since the Western Road presented such an animated appearance as it did on Thursday and Friday. Long before one o'clock, the appointed hour for the races to begin, it was thronged with vehicles of all kinds, from the two-horse carriages of the wealthier classes to the humble mule cart. The latter, of course, being filled to overflowing, which occasioned in one or two instances an unmistakable breakdown, to the no small discomfort of the passengers.

The omnibus was in requisition, and there were also hundreds of pedestrians, consisting of soldiers, jolly tars, artisans, and women, besides a number of equestrians; and those who preferred a water conveyance went down in boats. At one o'clock on Thursday, a bell was rung for the purpose of clearing the course. After which, the cavalry call was sounded on the bugle. Colonel Whitfield's Zonave and Dr. Boulton's Alina competed for the Nassau Cup, valued £20. 5s., which was won by Zonave.

The proceeds of the Thursday and Friday races were given to the Lancashire Relief Fund (£102. 4s. 4d.).

It is also interesting to note that all horse racing events were noted to be under the distinguished patronage of a royal governor throughout the 1800s--very, very interesting!

The *Nassau Guardian*
and Bahama Islands

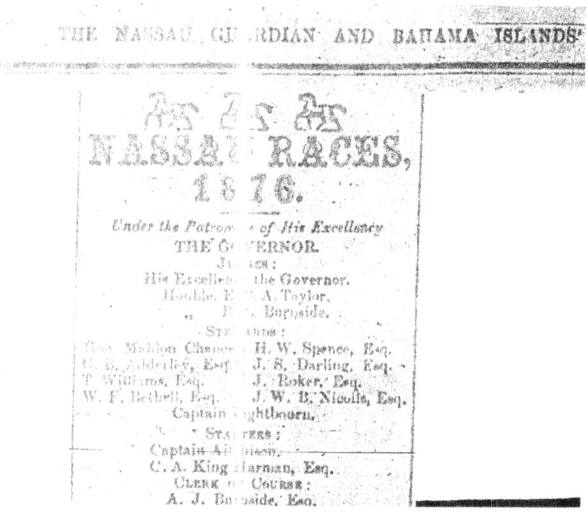

Nassau Races,

1876

Under the patronage of His Excellency
the Governor.

JUDGES:
His Excellency the Governor
Honorable E. B. A. Taylor
B. L. Burnside

STEWARDS:

Hon. Mahlon Chance   H. W. Spence, Esq.
G. B. Adderley, Esq.   J. S. Darling, Esq.
T. Williams, Esq.   J. Roker, Esq.
W. F. Bethell, Esq.   J. W. B. Nicolls, Esq.
                Captain Lightbourn

STARTERS:

Captain Aitchison
C. A. King Harnian, Esq.

CLERK OF THE COURSE:
A. J. Burnside, Esq.

PUBLIC AUCTION

R.W. Farrington

WILL SELL
on Thursday, the 1st Day April Next
in the Vendue House,
at 11:00 O'clock

That fine Family Residence, the property of the late
Sir William H. Doyle situated in West Hill Street and at
present occupied by the Rev C. C. WakeField.

Sold per order of the Executive

TERMS made Known at time of sale, Nassau,
24th March, 1880

March 30, 1881

Easter Races,
under the patronage of His Excellency
the Governor,
will take place at the racecourse, which has been kindly loaned for
the occasion, on Monday, the eighteenth
of April 1881, at one o'clock.

STEWARDS:

Hon. E. B. A. Taylor	Dr. Major
Hon. W. A. M. Sheriff	R. W. Farrington
Hon. Capt. Foster	Gen. B. Adderley
Lieut. Brady	J. S. Darling
Lieut. Warner	T. A. Thompson
Capt. Coppinger	J. B. Brown

Vincent Mathew

JUDGE:
Hon. W. A. M. Sheriff

STARTERS:
Capt. Foster and Lieut. Brady
CLERK OF THE COURSE:
Dr. Major

REGULATIONS.

Entries must be [illegible]de to the Stewards on Wednesday, th[illegible] 23rd, between the hours of one and two o'clock, at the Public Buildings. [illegible]e horse to be present at the time of ent[illegible] for the Stewards' inspection. Parties entering horses to declare their colours.

The second horse in a race to save a stake.

Time between heats, 20 minutes; the race to commence at one o'clock.

The Newmarket Rules will be observed, and the decision of the Stewards final.

ENTRAN[illegible]E FEES:

Horses over 14 hands	10s.
Island Ponies	5s.
Mules	2s.
Donkeys	1s.

Carriages will be admitted to the Race Course at 1s. per whee[illegible] on the day of the races.

Equestrians	2s.
Foot Passengers	6d.

A fee of £1 will be charged for all horses, &c. training over the [illegible]assau Course.

Feby. 2, 1876.

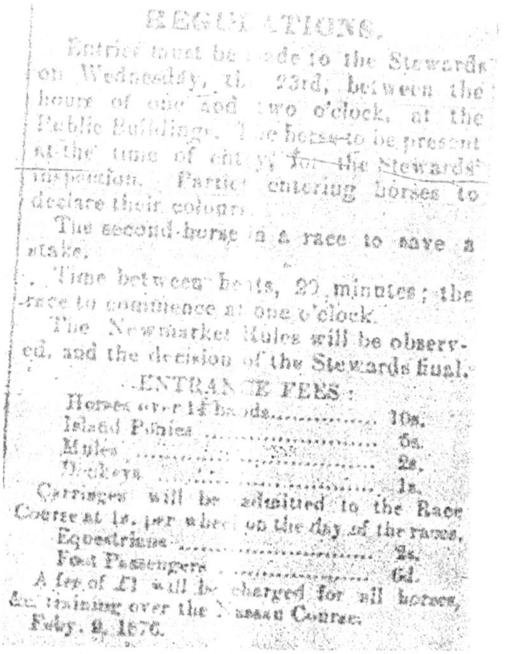

REGULATIONS

Carriages will be admitted to the course at 6d. per wheel.

Pedestrians, 6d.

Equestrians, 1s.

Tickets for the grandstand can be obtained at the store of Messrs. Brown and Musgrove.

The entrance fees to be paid on the date of entrance.

The amount of purses to be run for will be made known in another issue.

14 March 1881

Just received from New York:

Tins roast beef, tins deviced meats,
tins boneless pigs' feet.

John S. George & Co.

30 March 1881.

1881 Easter Monday Races from the *Nassau Guardian* Special Correspondent

On Monday, between the hours of twelve and one o'clock, the road leading to the west presented a rather annual and lively appearance. Pedestrians, equestrians, and vehicles of every conceivable shape and form crowded along the Queen's Highway, all moving toward the common destination, the Hobby Horse Hall Racecourse; and everyone in the vehicle accepted appeared to be thoroughly enjoying himself, from the gentleman, quietly seated in his carriage, to the laborer, somewhat uncomfortably bumped and tossed about on the seat of his donkey cart.

At about 1:30 PM at the call of the bugle, three horses entered upon the course, viz., Mr. Vincent F. Mathew's Maximilian Stuart, Mr. Brown's Ida, and Mr. Stanley Adderley's Dollie. This was the race of the day, and the cup was to be presented by Mr. John Brown. The jockeys, having mounted, it was at once seen that great difficulty would be experienced in affecting a start. (The first time the term *jockey* was applied to the riders.) Owing to the restiveness of both Dollie and Ida, these two horses were again and again brought up by their riders, but as often, they did refuse to start, and it was during one of those attempts that the horses rushed off without the flag being dropped. The official starter says they knew not why, and the jockeys confessed that they knew not how. However, Maximilian Stuart and Ida obtained by this freak start about two clear lengths of Dollie, who, nevertheless, to the surprise of everyone, recovered this disadvantage at the western turn of the course; and before the gate had been reached, she took the lead and kept it up during the remainder of the way, passing the judges stand first about two lengths, Maximilian Stuart being second, and Ida last.

The starters, having stated that they had given no signal, the judge declared, in accordance with the rules of the Turf Club, that there was no race, and the horses must compete again for the cup.

On this occasion, a good start was effected. Ida came in first amid great cheering and no small excitement, Maximilian Stuart, second, and Stanley Adderley's Dollie, last!

In the second race, there were Ida, now a general favorite, Maximilian Stuart, and R. W. Farrington's Banco. This race Ida also won.

Hobby Hall Racecourse was also used by the West Indian Regiment to race their ponies and to keep them fit for over fifty years. Finally, in 1893, the West Indian Regiment left the Bahamas, and the first group of West Indian Police Recruit arrived from Barbados to help the local constable's police the colony of the Bahamas. They were called constabularies.

1900-1901 the citizens of the Bahamas was lottery mad in playing the numbers game and the Bay Street merchants saw this as an economic drain on their business and they sought help from their representative in the House of Assembly.

To enact a law to act as a deterrent so the citizens of the Bahamas will not engage in operating a lottery. It is interesting to note that it was not the Christian Churches of the Bahamas; it was the Bay Street merchants, to object

More on this gaming matter in the Author's note!

The merchants of Nassau never opposed horse racing. The John S. George's, R. R. Farrington, the Kelly's, Damianos, the Pritchards, Christofilis, the Tilliaco's Christies, Malcolm's, Sands, Roberts, Symonette's, Maura's, Dupuch's, Chipman's, Darville's, Sawyer's, Thompson's, Bethel's, Baker's, Pinder's, Grammaticos, Brice's, Adderley's, Mailis, Jones, Bakers, French & Armoury.

At the turn of the century, racing continued at Hobby Horse Hall, and at the beginning of World War I in 1914, the Sporting Seat was closed after 119 years. Oriental Park Racetrack opened in Havana, Cuba, in 1915. The war ended in 1918, and Hobby Horse Hall reopened in 1921 by Mr. H. N. Chipman. Hialeah Racetrack in Miami, Florida, opened in 1925, and it was told that all the whisky was brought in from Nassau to add to the celebrations.

Evil spirits consignment of Booze Nassau N.P. Bahamas 1921.

The historical survey of the land indicated that by virtue of a number of devices, parcels or fractions of the land were purchased from 1835 by different persons. It was not until the twentieth of October 1932 that the whole track was conveyed by a Mr. Frank Munson to Sir Bede E. Clifford, governor of the Bahama Islands.

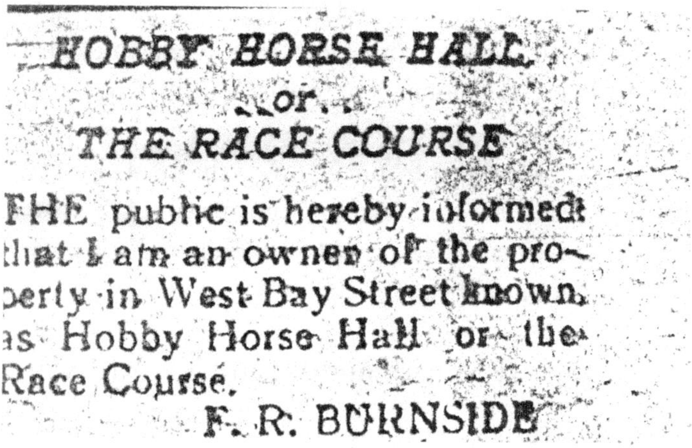

HOBBY HORSE HALL,
or
THE RACE COURSE

FHE public is hereby informed
that I am an owner of the property in West Bay Street known,
as Hobby Horse Hall or the
Race Course.

F. R. BURNSIDE

1921
Hobby Horse Hall
or
the Racecourse

The public is hereby informed that I am an owner of the property
in West Bay Street known as Hobby Horse Hall or the Racecourse.

F. R. Burnside

Mr. Frank Munson's family owned the Munson's Shipping Co. Their cruise ships sailed weekly from New York to Bermuda to Nassau. They actually were the pioneers of tourism to the Bahamas.

A horse racing bill was introduced in parliament, by Mr. Walter Young, and passed, and the Racing Commission Act was gazetted, and now the Bahamas government was prepared for government-supervised pari-mutuel betting.

Government-supervised pari-mutuel betting started with a five-pound (£5) bet.

ALLAN ROBERTS AND "ARAB"

On March 24, 1933, the local press announced that the late Allan Roberts had challenged the late H. N. Chipman to race his polo pony, King, against the challenger's pride, Arab.

POLO CLUB ARRANGES HORSERACES

BLUE RIBBON AND DERBY EVENTS

DETAILS OF PROGRAMME

A Blue ribbon race for horses owned by club members will be one of the features of the horse races to be held on the old race course on Empire day by the Nassau Amateur Polo Association competing in the event. Two heats will be run, the winners to run against each other in a final race.

Besides this event and a Derby race for a purse between horses owned by Messrs. H. N. Kelly, H. N. Chipman, Alan Roberts and A. B. Malcolm, there will be races for horses, mules and donkeys. In the race for carriage horses, a first prize of £5 and a second prize of £1, will be given, while in the race for dray horses there will be a first prize of £3 and a second of 15s.

A mule race, with £2 for the first prize and 10s. for the second, and a donkey race--with three prizes of 15s., 10s. and 5s. respectively, will also be held.

All entries for the races must be in not later than Saturday, May 20th, at noon, and a charge of 4s. for each horse and 2s. for each mule entered will be made, donkeys being allowed to enter free of charge.

The entrance fee to the course will be 1s. a person with an additional charge of 2s. for every carriage and 4s. for every car.

Although the original wager was for five pounds (£5), the papers reported it to be one hundred pounds (£100)--no mean sum in those days--and interest in the race erupted!

Other horse owners and members of the Nassau Amateur Polo Association decided that they would like to put their mounts against one another, and plans were soon being laid for a full day of racing. No class of animal was excluded. There were events for carriage horses, drays, mules, and donkeys.

Two more polo players came forward to race with Mr. Roberts and Mr. Chipman--A. B. Malcolm with Kanaka and H. N. Kelly with Sansovina.

Entries and Riders

Kanaka, 125 pounds, ridden by Sidney Pyfrom; Sansovina, 141 pounds, ridden by Harcourt Maura; King, 155 pounds, ridden by C. C. Halliday; and Arab, ridden by Allan Roberts.

The date was set for Empire Day, May 24, at the old track, Hobby Horse Hall.

At the time the Polo Association took it over for its meet, the track was unused for over twelve years, with brush and undergrowth reducing the course to a mere path. A one-day gaming permit was granted.

The government supplied a team of laborers from the Nassau prison, and under the direction of members of the association, the track was cleared and graded for the race.

PROGRAMME AND ENTRIES FOR EMPIRE DAY HORSE RACES

Administrator to See Events

Widespread interest is being taken in the horse races which will be held at Montagu Park Race Course on Empire Day, starting at 1 p.m., by the Nassau Polo Association, under the distinguished patronage of His Excellency the Administrator and the Hon. Mrs. Charles Dundas, who will witness the events.

Interest centres particularly in the "Derby" event, in which four of the finest horses in the island will compete. Time nor money is being spared to prepare these horses for the event, and not infrequently they are out long before daylight for training and in order to get their time when spying eyes are not around. It has been stated that all the horses, excepting one, can make the course in 2 minutes, the other making it in 2.5, but it is said that this horse is quickest on the get-away and it may be possible for him to get a clear field while the others are jostling for position.

The following is the programme and list of entries:

1. **Nassau Polo Team:**
   Johnny Sears "Saracen".
   A. W. Brooks. "Sheik".
   Cory Damianos. "Black Lady".
   A. K. Cole. "Deuce".
   J. French. "Rex".

2. **Carriage Class:**
   C. A. Fox. "Jim".
   E. Munnings. "Nelson".
   E. Cummings. "Chance".
   D. Francis. "Roland".
   A. Griffiths. "Callawood".

3. **Bahamas Derby.**
   A. B. Malcolm's "Kanaka", Sidney Pyfrom up.
   H. N. Chipman's "King", Commander C. C. Halliday up.
   A. Roberts's "Arab", A. Roberts up.
   H. N. Kelly's "Sansovina," Harcourt Maura up.

4. **Dray Class:**
   D. Lindsay. "Blues".
   G. W. Knowles. "Star".
   S. N. Smith. "Peter Pan".
   Herbert Barr. "Rex".
   Cecil Davis. "Bill".

5. **Mule Class:**
   Adam Johnson. "Adam".
   S. Cockburn. "Evie".
   Charles Chatham. "Breezy".

6. **Donkey race** (free for all).

7. **Special race** between Mr. A. B. Malcolm's "Kanaka", Mr. Cory Damianos's "Black Lady", and Mr. C. A. Fox's "Jim".

Seabury Will Not Stand for Mayor

Hobby Horse Hall

Poem

The Tribune
By Meklub
May 24, 1933

Oh! tough were the riders who rode
for a fall,
In the old days, the bold days at
Hobby Horse Hall,
And game were the ponies from pad-
dock and stall,
And fair were the ladies who came
one and all
To show off their laces and their
pretty faces
At the old Nassau races at Hobby
Horse Hall.

But what of the jockeys who'll
answer the call
Of "steady," "get ready" at Hobby
Horse Hall?
When *King* and *Kanaka* and *Arab*
and all
Line up at the post for the ribbon
to fall,
They'll cut loose the traces and
show us their paces

In next Wednesday's races at Hobby
Horse Hall.

Good Luck to the ponies, the big
ones and small,
Good Luck to the riders at Hobby
Horse Hall.
Good Luck to the men who are going
to install
An up-to-date track so that we,
one and all,
Can shut up our places, forget our
disgraces,
And be off to the races at Hobby
Horse Hall.

On Empire Day, all of Nassau turned out. Admittance was one shilling for individuals and four shillings for cars, with no limit on the number of passengers.

HOBBY HORSE HALL
DERBY RACE
WEDNESDAY MAY 21, 1931
WINNER KASAKA
JOCKEY & TRAINER SIDNEY PYFROM
OWNER A.B. MALCOLM

Big Boy Ferguson   Sidney Pyfrom

Kanaka, Mr. A. B. Malcolm's powerful stallion, ran to victory in the Bahamas derby whilst a thousand voices cheered his magnificent stride; H. N. Kelly's Sansovina came in second; Mr. H. N. Chipman's King, third; Arab lost his saddle in the back stretch and came in last.

Kanaka came from Exuma, sired by Desmond, one of the two Thoroughbred horses imported from Jamaica by the late C. E. Bethell.

The second big event of the day was the polo team's half mile, which was declared no race because the riders did not go back to the stand for identification following the race. Among those running in this event were Reginald Farrington's Uncle Dodie, A. K. Cole's Deuce, A. R. Braynen's Broker's Tip, and W. J. French's Rex.

So successful was the meet that the Fort Montagu Beach Hotel owner and managing director, Mr. George Murphy, took out a lease on the land and made application for a jockey club license in the name of Montagu Park Racing Association to the government to operate a racetrack with government-supervised pari-mutuel betting, and it was granted. Mr. Murphy immediately began renovations of the historic Hobby Horse Hall Racecourse, and he announced its opening date of January 24, 1934.

Memories, the compelling powers
of auld acquaintance; and the
threads that bind us to some place
called home.

Hobby Horse Hall!

Go out upon the shady side of
Bay Street and whisper to the
merchant at his door the *open se-
same* of this good ancient name.

The smile that happy recollec-
tion brings will overspread his
face; pictures of olden gaities will
fill his mind; stories his father told
will once more fill his ears; and the
fresh vigour of a vanished youth
will invigorate his voice and he will
speak again of *Blucher* young Mc-
Pherson rode, when T. B. Thompson brought him from Jamaica, or
of the speed of that fast filly
"Grace Darling," or the size of
"Spanker."

And if he was a jockey, when a
lad, he'll tell you of the races he
would ride when there were soldiers in the Nassau Forts.

For this name takes a man a
long way back to those far days
when George the Fourth was King
and Nelson drove the Frenchmen
from the Western seas.

Hobby Horse Hall!

It is a name that rolls upon the
tongue and brings a cheerful picture to the mind.

Why change it then for some
inappropriate name, that has no
association with the west or with
the historic race course?

53

HOBBY HORSE HALL.

Many of our readers have expressed themselves as being very much opposed to changing the old name "Hobby Horse Hall" to Montagu Park but few of them know how long this quaint name has been associated with the racecourse site. The origin of the name is doubtless lost in antiquity but goes back well over a century and probably much longer for it is referred to in letters written from Nassau in 1824 and the fact that there was no large building then on the estate suggests that the estate might have been owned and probably named by one of the Loyalist settlers at least a hundred and fifty years ago and that the original homestead had been destroyed.

In the letters, written by a visitor to Nassau in the winter of 1823-24 and published in 1827, this writer (said to be a Miss Hart) described a party at The "Hut" or "Hobby Horse Hall." "The house stands on a wide plain far from the road, it is a thatched cottage built merely for marooning parties contains but two rooms and has a piazza; it is surrounded on all sides at a distance by low trees or a kind of forest underbrush and flowers bloom amidst the rocks and stones with wonderful prodigality. . . . When we drove away from the scene of so much gaiety and turned to take a last look at the Hut, I thought I could have been satisfied to pass my whole life there. It stood so alone from all the world, the ocean alone seemed near, and no vestige of a habitation wasted seen and no trace that could say the hand of man had been there."

Mr. Murphy changed the name of the historic track to Montagu Park, and the Bahamian residents were very upset with his decision. They contended that there was too much history behind the name Hobby Horse Hall, and it should not be changed. It was a name that rolled upon the tongue and brought a cheerful picture to the mind, for this name took a man a long way back to those far days when George IV was king and Nelson drove the Frenchmen from the Western Seas.

To this day there is no recorded information as to who built the historic racecourse. Was it really Governor Dunmore (1787–1796)?

On a Wednesday afternoon at 2:30 PM, January 1934, Montagu Park Racetrack opened under the distinguished patronage of His Excellency, Sir Bede Clifford, and Lady Clifford.

OPENING DAY AT MONTAGU PARK.

DISTINGUISHED GATHERING AT RACE TRACK.

FAVOURITES GIVE PLACE TO LONG PRICED OUTSIDERS.

Considering that only three months ago the whole of this area was a wilderness and considering that all the people engaged in the conduct of the races are performing their duties for the first time the whole afternoon has been a tremendous success. Such was the verdict of His Excellency the Governor during the running of the events at the opening meet of Montagu Park Race Track.

It may be said that one of the most indefatigable workers for the success of the afternoon was the Governor himself. He acted as starter, was in the paddock at the saddling of the horses and weighing-in of the jockeys and on the judges' stand during the races.

The races themselves were exciting and the feature of the day, which gave the excitement, and brought sorrow and joy in its train, was the fact that in almost every instance the long priced outsiders beat the favourites.

The first race, timed to start, at two-thirty, did not get away from the half mile post on the north side of the track until after three and by that time's gathering of some thousand people were seated in the club house, the grandstand, or for the most part moving between the paddock, the pari-mutuel, or the notice board, on the far side of the rails, opposite the Club house.

One outstanding feature of the day was the way in which the pari-mutuel windows were patronised. Everybody seemed to want to have a stake on something and before and after each race the clerks at the windows were kept busy taking in bets or paying out profits. It was remarkable how smoothly and satisfactorily the betting was managed.

The day's events started well with a win, most appropriately, for Mrs. George Murphy's Chance. As the ponies went to the half-mile starting post on the north side of the track the band in the grandstand played stirring music and the starting odds stood at 3-2 Chance, 6-1 Black Lady and Rex, 14-1 Champion and Water Knight with Bill at 17-1 and the other two, Matchum and Bluey, at 35-1.

The ponies got away to a good start and came round the curve in a bunch. As they came down the straight it could be seen that Chance and Black Lady were in a close lead with Rex coming up behind. It was a splendid finish, the first two horses coming almost neck and neck until Chance passed the post half a length ahead. Rex finished third three lengths behind. The time of the four furlongs was 1 minute four seconds.

Result: Chance, jockey Brennan. First: 10s. 3d.; 9s. 3d., 6s. 3d.
Black Lady, jockey Evans. Second. 16s. 3d., 8s. 6d.
Rex, jockey Smith. Third 6s.
Chance, owned by Mrs. Geo. Murphy; Black Lady by Cory Donnalson; Rex by N. J. French.

It was a popular win and both Mrs. Murphy and Mr. Murphy came in for many congratulations.

The second race for Bahamian breds, six furlongs, provided one of the greatest thrills of the day. It had an added interest in that it was the first half of the Daily Double. At the paddock it seemed that no one had any doubt but that the race lay between Tricks and Sansovino although Playboy came in for a good share of notice. The starting odds bore out this impression for the horses went down to the six furlong post at the north-east corner of the track priced as follows: Tricks 3-2, Sansovina 4-1, Defiance 8-1, Playboy 16-1 Saraband 16-1, and Kanaka 33-1.

At the starting post Saraband caused a sensation by getting out of control and running away with her jockey Brennan. He did the complete round of the track before he joined the other horses at the post.

A roar from the excited spectators on the Grandstand announced that the horses were off and they could be seen coming along the northern straight in good style. As they rounded the bend and came into the straight the excitement became intense for it was seen that Playboy was leading with the orange and black stripes of Mr. A. B. Malcolm's outsider Kanaka coming up and gaining on her. Tricks was coming up and it was obvious that the finish was going to be close. As they passed the grandstand Kanaka drew ahead and won by a close margin, Tricks third. The time was 1 minute thirty seconds.

Result: Kanaka, jockey Carroll. First. £8 8s. 3d., 14s. 9d., 8s. 3d.
Playboy, jockey McPhee. Second. 12s. 9d., 7s. 6d.
Tricks, jockey Evans. Third 7s.
Kanaka owned by A. B. Malcolm.
Playboy, Moore-Malcolm stable.
Tricks, the Hon. Q. H. Curry.

It was a splendid race and Playboy might have brought it off had Mc-Phee held him a little and had not broken his whip.

The third race maintained the excitement. Hallmark, Mr. D. J. DeGregory, and Day Break, Mr. R. R. Farrington, started favourites. Brooke-Carlisle had been unnoticed at 67-1.

The race started from the five furlong post at a fast pace and it was soon noticeable that Brooke-Carlisle carrying the black and white colours of Mrs. Etienne Dupuch was bidding fair to upset the odds. This prognostication was verified as the bunch came into the straight, for F. Bowe brought his horse to the front and kept him there until the post was passed. Time, 1 minute and 15 seconds.

Result: Brooke-Carlisle, jockey F. Bowe. First £4. 6s. 3d., £2. 11s. 3d., 10s. 6d.
Lady May, jockey Brennan. Second. 15s., 9s. 9d.
Jane Mc., jockey Clarke. Third. £1. 8s. 6d.

Brooke-Carlisle, Mrs. Etienne Dupuch, Lady May, Capt. Weech. Jane Mc. Mrs G. Murphy.

There were several lucky backers who took both these long prices.

The fourth race, brought the favourite home. The starting odds were Sheik 3-1, Jim 3-1, Rouge et Noir, Arab and Eclipse 6-1, Rob Roy 11-1, Prince 14-1, Nelson 67-1. Sheik led the procession all round the four furlongs and finished in 1 minute, 1 second with Arab and Jim second and third.

Result: Sheik, jockey Clarke. First. £1 4s. 0d., 8s. 9d., 6s.
Arab, jockey Brennan. Second. 13s. 9d.
Jim, jockey Turnquest. 6s. 3d.
Sheik, Alva Brooks; Arab, Allan Roberts; Jim, C. A. Fox.

The fifth race, the inaugural handicap for five year olds and upwards, for thoroughbreds, was the second race of the daily double and had there been anyone with the foresight or ingenuity or plain luck to have spotted both the winners they would have been in luck indeed, for once again the long outsider came home. It was getting towards dusk when His Excellency the Governor mounted the starters' stand in front of the judges' box and the horses lined up. From conversations overheard at the saddling ring it seemed as though the race must lie between Dirty Dick and Jane Mc. but experience had proved

by this time that the favourites were not coming home on this day.

His Excellency the Governor proved himself a capable starter and sent the tape up with very little delay. Lord Conroy led all the way. It had become so dark that it was impossible to follow the horses on the far side of the track but they came down the home stretch Lord Conroy, Fedafire and Jane Mc., third.

The starting odds had placed the horses as follows: Jane Mc. 3-2, Durran 6-1, Fedafire 9-1, Dirty Dick 14-1, Lord Conroy 20-1, but the finishing results showed Lord Conroy jockey Clarke. First. £7. 11s. 0d., £1 16s. 6d., £1 0s. 3d. Fedafire, jockey Evans. Second. £1 7s. 6d., 3s. 6d.; Jane Mc., jockey Marlin, third. 6s. 9d.

Lord Conroy, Mr. A. H. Sands; Fedafire, Mr. A. H. Sands; Jane Mc. W. Brice Pinder.

A curious feature of this race was that owing to the desire of the public to get bets on it the pari-mutuel were unable to take them all in and some fifty people were turned away as the race was on before they could place their money.

It had become so dark by this time that the races had to be abandoned. The late start and a certain slowness which will undoubtedly remedy itself as the grooms and jockeys get accustomed to the routine of racing had thrown the programme out of time. It might be suggested that the numbers of the horses are placed on both sides of the saddle so that the horses may be recognised as they go up and down past the grandstand and the Club house.

It was a difficult matter in the continual movement of the throng from the clubhouse and grandstand to the saddling ring and the pari-mutuel windows to notice everybody but almost everybody was there.

His Excellency the Governor with the Honble. Lady Clifford brought Sir Griffith and Lady Boynton, Mr. John Gundry and Mr. John Gundry, Jr. in their party, which included Mmle. Rebold, Captain Houstoun-Boswall and Captain Mintje Wilson also.

Captain Houstoun-Boswall with Mr. John Burnside, Mr. Newell Kelly and the Hon. A. K. Cole acted as judges.

His Grace the Duke of Sutherland came from Old Fort with Commander Edmonstone and party, His Honour the Chief Justice and Mrs. Tute, the Hon. Sir George and Lady Johnson; the Hon. Walter K. Moore and Mrs. Moore; the Hon. O. H. Curry, the Hon. R. G. Collins, Miss Collins, the Hon. Harcourt and Mrs. Malcolm, Dr. and Mrs. Percy Malcolm, Lady Williams-Taylor, Mr. and Mrs. George Murphy, Mr. and Mrs. Russell Gulpe, Mr. and Mrs. Harold Strebigh, Dr. and Mrs. Graham, Commander and Miss Langton-Jones, Mr. R. H. Curry, Dr., and Mrs. Dolley, Mr. and Mrs. B. K. Graham, Miss Adderley, Mrs. C. Harley Moseley and Mr. B. J. Graham, were amongst those present but it was very difficult to notice every one.

Mr. Irving Berlin had come over from Westbourne and enjoyed himself immensely in trying to pick the winners and failing every time. He shared his bets with a friend, each putting as he termed it "two and a half shillings" on the tote.

The whole afternoon's racing was well organised and everybody was thoroughly well pleased, especially Mr. Charles Reader of the Jungle orchestra who, as rumour had it, was among the lucky ones.

First Race Entries:

Purse: £25
Distance: four furlongs
Minimum weight: ninety pounds

	Odds	Jockey
(1) Bill	17–1	Clarke
(2) Matchum	35–1	-
(3) Black Lady	14–1	Evans
(4) Champion	17–1	S. Pyfrom
(5) Water Night	17–1	Marlin
(6) Rex	14–1	Smith
(7) Chance	3–2	Brennan
(8) Blues	35–1	Carrol

They're OFF!

Bare footed Bahamian jockey's are seen during the start at Hobby Horse Hall.

Elegantly dress racing fans are seen in merriment of excitement cheering the winning horse.

The first race was won by Mrs. George Murphy's Chance, ridden by Brennan; Black Lady, second; and Rex, third.

It may be said that one of the most indefatigable workers for the success of the afternoon was the governor himself. He acted as starter, was in the paddock at the saddling of the horses and weighing in of its jockeys, and on the judges' stand during the races.

One outstanding feature of the day was the way in which the parimutuel windows were patronized. It was remarkable how smoothly and satisfactorily its betting was managed! It is also interesting to note that it was the beginning of the most popular tourist attraction in the colony of the Bahamas. (You never know what you've got until you lose it!)

At the Finish Line

Royal Visitors at the Races

The Right Honorable the Earl of Athlone and Her Royal Highness Princess Alice, Countess of Athlone, were the guests of the governor, Sir Bede Clifford, and Lady Clifford at Montagu Park Racecourse on Friday, February 2, 1934. The Earl of Athlone was governor-general of South Africa from 1923 to 1931 and is the younger brother of Queen Mary.

H. R. H. Princess Alice, Countess of Athlone.

Royal Visitors at Hialeah Park, Miami, Florida

The royal guests on Saturday, February 17, 1934, which was marked by the first official visit of British royalty to Florida, witnessed the running of the first Bahamas Handicap Race, sponsored by the Nassau Development Board. The seven-furlong race was won by Time Supply, sired by Timemaker, and ridden by Don Meade. Mrs. F. A. Garreaud, owner of the fast three-year-old, graciously accepted the trophy cup from Sir Bede Clifford. The royal party was entertained at the Palm Beach mansion of Mr. Widner, owner of Hialeah Park Course, before returning to Nassau. The Bahamas Handicap Race still remains an annual event.

PRICE 2d.

LAST MEET OF SEASON.

FRIDAY'S RACES

The following are the nominations for the 12th meeting at the Montagu Park Race Track to be held next Friday afternoon.

First Race. 3 Furlongs.
1. Mischief (Mrs. R. T. Symonette) 105. Turnquest.
2. Peter Pan (S. N. Smith) 100. Glynton.
3. Beauty. (Errol Johnson) 100. Braynen.
4. Breeze. (Malcolm-Moore) 105. McPhee.
5. Jane M. (Mrs. Murphy) 105. Clarke.
6. Lady Mark. (De Gregory Bros.) 100. Smith.
7. Arab (Allan Roberts) 100. Cooper.

Second Race. 6 Furlongs. Bahamias Derby £30 added.
1. Tricks. (Hon. O. H. Curry) 115. Rowe.
2. Kanaka (Malcolm-Moore) 100. Turnquest.
3. King (H. N. Chipman) 107. Sweeting.
4. Sassorina. (Cory Damianos) 100. Smith.
5. Defiance. (Mrs. Murphy) 100. Cooper.
6. Confusion. (Mrs. Murphy) 105. Glynton.
7. Chieftain. (Malcolm-Moore) 105. Fox.
8. Sheik. (Alva Brook) 100. Clarke.
9. Brooks Carlisle (Mrs. E. Dupuch) 107. Brennan.
10. Play Boy. (Malcolm-Moore) 125. McPhee.

Third Race. 4 Furlongs.
1. Aleazar. (Malcolm-Moore) 100. Glynton.
2. Morning Dew. (Mrs. Murphy) 105. Braynen.
3. Hall Mark. (DeGregory Bros.) 105. Smith.
4. Lady May. (Mrs. Weech) 105. McPhee.
5. Rouge et Noir. (Mrs. R. T. Symonette) 100. Turnquest.
6. Black Lady. (Cory Damianos) 100. Cooper.
7. Kismet. (A. F. Adderley) 105. Braynen.

Fourth Race.—4 Furlongs.
1. Chiquita (Mrs. McKinney) Glynton.
2. Water Knight (S. F. White) McPhee.
3. Square Deal (A. Lloyd) Smith.
4. Lassie. (Wm. Pendlebury) Clarke.
5. Star (R. Ingram) Fox.
6. Bill (C. Albury) Braynen.
7. Mixie (Pyfrom Bros.) Cooper.
8. Primo Carnera (Everette Sands) Carrol.

Fifth Race. 1 Mile.
1. Day Break (R. H. Farrington) 107. Smith.
2. Champion. (Pyfrom Bros.) 105. Fox.
3. Jim (C. A Fox) 100. Glynton.
4. Chance. (Mrs. Murphy) 105. Clarke.
5. Rex. (N. J. French) 103. Braynen.
6. Sarabatul (Miss Althea) 105. Cooper.

Sixth Race. 7 Furlongs.
1. Lord Conroy. (A. H. Sands) 117. Braynen.
2. Bluebeer (H. Chipan) 112. K. Carrel.
3. Fedaflee. A. H. Sands) 100. McPhee.
4. Jane Ma. (Wm. Brice Pinder) 107. Smith.
5. Durron (Wm. Brice Pinder) 110. Clarke.

The following order is merely tentative and will be corrected if necessary.

AMERICAN RACING ACES SAIL FOR ITALY.

New York, April 9.—Peter de

Nassau Guardian

AND BAHAMA ISLANDS ADVOCATE AND INTELLIGENCER
ESTABLISHED 1844.

NASSAU, BAHAMAS, SATURDAY, FEBRUARY 17, 1934.

PRICE 3d.

SUCCESSFUL RACE MEET AT MONTAGU PARK.

LARGE NUMBERS WITNESS EXCITING RACES.

EVENTS FILMED BY NEWS REEL CAMERA MEN.

A large attendance to Clubhouse stand, Grandstand and on the rail witnessed some most exciting finishes yesterday at Montagu Park, and were photographed from various positions by the cameramen of the News Reels companies.

Before the start of the first race the pound wagon of the Paramount News was brought into the roadway outside the paddock and the horses and jockies were photographed in the ring being saddled, the jockies being weighed in. Mr. Cole called out the names of the jockies and their weights and then as the horses were walked round the paddock.

After that the cameras were taken to various parts of the course so that the start of the races the horses coming round the bend and down the straight, and close-up of the finish might be taken. Mr. Dixon told our representative that the cameramen had made one of the most complete coverage of any race meeting he had known.

A feature of yesterday's meet was the speedy manner in which Sergeant Major Hawkins got the horses away from the starting post. There was hardly any delay in any of the events.

The first race—four furlongs for Native ponies and a purse of £20—saw Black Lady start favourite. Re an even money. Silver 3-1, Ren 12-1, Ren and Charity 10-1, Square Measure 6-1, and Prince 20-1. Black Lady led from the start and held her position all the way with Ren and Square Measure fighting for place a few lengths behind. At the end Prince was running up fast but could not get into the money. Black Lady won in 1 minute and 5 6ths seconds with Ren 3 6ths of a second behind Square Measure did well for his owner Mrs. Harold Chipman by coming in third.

Result. 1. Black Lady (Roy Davidson) Clarke. Paid £6 10/9, 12/-.
2. Ren, (N. J. Francis) Smith. 17/9, 15/9.
3. Square Measure (Mrs. Harold Chipman) Glynton. £1 4s. 6d.

After the first race the club house stand began to fill up fast and soon there was the largest gathering, so historical, of all the four meetings.

The second race proved so victory for the backers of Mr. H. N. Chipman's black gelding King. Chief tain started favourite at 5-1. Lady ...

May 8-1, Defiance 5-1, King 7-1, Champion 10-1, Mudding Deer 20-1. This race for 3 years old and up. Prize furlongs for a purse of £15, won the first half of the Daily Double. King got away at the start and lead easily all round winning in 1 minute and 11 seconds from Chieftain, four 5ths of a second behind, and Defiance. The favourite did not show up at all.

Result. 1. King (H. N. Chipman) Bronson. £1 10s. 4d. 17/-, 6/9.
2. Chieftain (Maloney-Lowe) Carroll. 7/9, 7/-.
3. Defiance (Geo. George Murphy) Clarke. 8/3.

The third race for Bahamian Bred and Native Ponies afforded much speculation amongst the public. Tricks and Play Boy started favourite at 5-1, Kuosia and Brudie Carlisle 4-1, Shell 12-1, Confusion 22-1. Play Boy got away at the start with Brodie-Carlisle and Tricks third and the positions kept changing so fast until the horses came round the bend that it was difficult to follow which was where. Round the bend Play Boy took first place with Tricks trying hard to get ahead and Kuosia third. Glynton did a very clever piece of riding. He tried to get through on the rail but failed and so pulled his horse out and came up on Play Boy at a tremendous pace. It did not seem possible that he would catch him but Glynton seemed inspired to win and just on the post he lifted Tricks forward and won by the fraction of a nose, one fifth of a second being exact. Play Boy had been suffering from a swollen fetlock but is a splendid pony. Next year Mrs. Moore should do very well with him. Time of the race 1 min. 22 2-5sec.

Result. 1. Tricks, (Mrs. O. H. Curry) Glynton. 16/6, 7/6, 7/-.
2. Play Boy (Moore-Maloney) McEwen 9/-, 7/-.
3. Kuosia (Moore-Maloney) Carroll. 8/2.

Fourth Race. Native Figures. 4 years old and up. Four Furlongs. Defi cult with Water Knight started a hot favourite at Col. Bill and Bapo-lle 3s at 4-1. Daly 11-1, Nol-son and Star 50-1.

Bapo-lle-Banes lead the way round the bend, who had the outside position, only a fifth of a second behind Klemet, and Star in third place. Turngood tried hard to overcome Melboe ...

but couldn't make it in the distance. Times Bapo'-Banes 1 minute 5 and 3-5ths seconds, Water Knight 1 min. 6 secs.

Result. 1. Bapo'-Banes (Allan Roberts) McPhee. £3 11s. 17/6, 7/-.
2. Water Knight (C. A. Fox) Turngood 7/6, 6/-.
3. Star, (H. H. Ingraham) Smith, 7/6.

Fifth Race—first half of Daily Double. Bahamian Bred and Native Ponies. 3 years old and up. Four furlongs. Four Furlongs. Me thew was so interesting problem for the backers. Klemet started favourite at 2-1, Arab 4-1, Dawn 6-1, Chance 7-1, Mischief 8-1, Beauty 11-1, Eclipse 27-1.

Beauty lead at the start but was overtaken by Klemet and Arab and did not show at all. Klemet kept in the lead with Arab and Chance behind. Arab made a hard fight for the finish but Klemet went ahead and won in 1 minute 2-3 5ths seconds by 1/5th of a second.

Result. 1. Klemet (A. F. Adderley) Brennan.
2. Arab (Allan Roberts) Carroll.
3. Chance, (Mrs. G. Murphy) Clarke.

Daily Double, of which there were three winners, paid £16 19s. 5d.

Sixth Race—For Thoroughbreds and Bahamian Bred 4 years old and up. Purse £45. 1 mile flat.

Lord Conroy started at even money. Fedaire and Jane Mc. 5-1, Durou and Blucher (late Dirty Dick) 14-1.

A wire stall was erected in the first position for Jane Mc. who stood at the starting post quite contentedly holding the wire in her teeth. Blucher threw Carroll as he went to the post. Sergeant Hawkins got the horses away to splendid start with Jane McIntosh. At the eastern end Fedaire took the lead with Lord Conroy second and Jane Mc. dropped back to third place. This order held all round the mile and a good finish brought Fedaire home the winner. 1 minute and 49 seconds 1/5th second ahead of Lord Conroy. This is the fastest time made in this race so far.

Result. 1. Fedaire (A. F. Sands) Clarke. Paid £2 11s. 7/6, 5/-.
2. Lord Conroy, A. H. Sands. 51/6 ...
3. Jane Mc. (Wm. Brice Fleeting) F. Bruce, 5/-.

Closing Meet at Montagu Park

LAST MEET OF SEASON.

TO-DAY'S RACES.

The following are the nominations for the 12th meeting at the Montagu Park Race Track to be held this afternoon.

First Race, 3 Furlongs.
1. Mischief (Mrs. R. T. Symonette) 105 Turnquest.
2. Peter Pan (S. N. Smith) 100, Glynton.
3. Beauty, (Errol Johnson) 100, Braynen.
4. Breeze, (Malcolm-Moore) 105, McPhee.
5. Jane M. (Mrs. Murphy) 105, Clarke.
6. Lady Mack, (De Gregory Bros.) 100, Smith.
7. Arab (Allan Roberts) 100, Cooper.

Second Race, 6 Furlongs.
Bahamian Derby £30 added.
1. Tricks (Hon. O. H. Curry) 115, Rose.
2. Kamdin (Malcolm-Moore) 100, Turnquest.
3. King (H. N. Chipman) 107, Sweeting.
4. Sansevina, (Cory Damianos) 100, Smith.
5. Defiance (Mrs. Murphy) 100, Cooper.
6. Confusion, (Mrs. Murphy) 105, Glynton.
7. Chieftain (Malcolm-Moore) 105, Fox.
8. Sleek (Allan Brook) 100, Clarke.
9. Brooks Carlson (Mrs. E. Haynor) 107, Brennan.
10. Pier Bay (Malcolm-Moore) 125, McPhee.

Third Race, 4 Furlongs.
1. Alcatoe (Malcolm-Moore) 100, Glynton.
2. Morning Star (Mrs. Murphy) 105, Braynen.
3. Half Mast (De Gregory Bros.) 105, Smith.
4. Lady May, (Mrs. Veerh) 105, McPhee.
5. Range o' Nale (Mrs. R. T. Symonette) 105, Turnquest.
6. Black Lady (Cory Damianos) 100, Cooper.
7. Kismet (A. P. Adderley) 105, Braynen.

Fourth Race, 4 Furlongs.
1. Chiquita (Mrs. McKinney) Glynton.
2. Water Knight (S. P. White) McPhee.
3. Square Deal (A. Lloyd) Smith.
4. Lassie, (Wm. Pendlebury) Clarke.
5. Star (R. Ingram) Fox.
6. Bill (C. Albury) Braynen.
7. Mizle (Pyfrom Bros.) Cooper.
8. Prime Carnera (Everette Sands) Carrol.

Fifth Race, 1 Mile.
1. Day Break (R. R. Farrington) 107, Smith.
2. Champion (Pyfrom Bros.) 105, Fox.
3. Jim (C. A. Fox) 100, Glynton.
4. Chance (Mrs. Murphy) 104, Clarke.
5. Rex (N. J. French) 104, Braynen.
6. Saraband (Miss Althea) 105, Cooper.

Sixth Race, 7 Furlongs.
1. Lord Conroy (A. H. Sands) 117, Braynen.
2. Bluefer (H. Chipman) 112, K. Carrol.
3. Foxfire, (A. H. Sands) 105, McPhee.
4. Jane Me. (Wm. Brice Pinder) 107, Smith.
5. Durron (Wm. Brice Pinder) 110, Clarke.

The following order is merely tentative and will be corrected if necessary.

65

Lady Dupuch with her prize-winning horse, Brooks Carlisle, holding the Govenor's trophy that Brooks had won at the Hobby Horse Hall.

Season ends with exciting program.

Season ends: A. F. Adderley's Kismet disqualified in second race.

Mr. George Murphy was very ecstatic with the interest well maintained throughout the twelve races meet at Montagu Park during the 1934 season.

Leading Jockey was C. Brennen with ten wins. Jockey Clarke and McPhee were running up with eight and seven wins respectfully. The Murphy stables captured the title for most wins.

In 1935, Lady Dupuch's Brooks Carlisle won the Duke of Kent Cup due to disqualification of Playboy. An unfortunate incident occurred during the running of the race for the Duke of Kent's Cup. Playboy romped in an easy winner only to be disqualified for fouling Forget-Me-Not. Hundreds of pounds were bet on Playboy, a strong favorite, and it is to be regretted that such an unfortunate incident should occur in the most important race of the year.

At Montagu Park, Sir John Maffee, Permanent Under-Secretary of State for the Colonies, presenting the second prize for thoroughbreds to Mrs. Kingsbury Moore and Mr. George Murphy. At the left Mr. Alfred Malcolm is holding the Duke of Kent's Trophy for thoroughbreds, with which he had been presented a moment before

At Montagu Park, Sir John Maffee, Permanent Under-Secretary of State for the Colonies, presenting the second prize for thoroughbreds to Mrs. Kingsbury Moore and Mr. George Murphy. *At the left* Mr. Alfred Malcolm is holding the Duke of Kent's Trophy for thoroughbreds, with which he had been presented a moment before

In 1936, A. B. Malcolm's Kanaka, ridden by Rupert Jenoure, won the most prestigious Duke of Kent Cup. Jockey Jenoure continued his exceptional riding by booting home three winners on the last day of the meet and thereby established himself definitely as the leading jockey of the season with ten (10) wins, in spite of an early four-week suspension.

The Murphy stables ended the season as the leading winner with ten (10) victories.

View from the Grand Stand

View of the horses parading in front of the
Grand Stand and Club House.

The horse is king now that another race season has opened at Montagu Park.

They're off

The horse is king now that another race season has opened at Montagu Park.

Brave Mark a thoroughbred stallion from the stable of Mr. Charles E. Bethell. This famous horse is the sire of many well-known race horses.

Jane Mac favourite thoroughbred owned by Mr. W. Brice Pinder.

Lord Conroy whose owner Mr. Arthur H. Sands has won many races with this beautiful thoroughbred.

The Shiek a native pony owned by Mr. Alva Brook.

In 1937, Montagu Park Racecourse opens with a canter. The first Tuesday racing was introduced by management to add to the winter tourist attraction. Tuesday and Friday, post time at 2:30 PM.

THE NASSAU GUARDIAN SATURDAY MARCH 13 1917

His Excellency the Governor as he appeared in presenting the Duke
of Kent's Cup to Mr. Fred Smith owner of "Wild Fire" after his victory
in the 100 guineas event on the 25th Feb.

His Excellency the Governor Sir Bede Clifford presents trophy
to Mr. Fred Smith owner of the winning horse "Wild Fire"

Mr. Fred Smith's Wild Fire won the one hundred guinea Duke of Kent's Cup. March 19, Wild Fire wins twice in sensational finishes. Montagu Park ends fourth season. Calamity, owned by Basil Smith and ridden by Sidney Pyfrom, wins twice, including the Montagu Park Gentleman's Cup Race. World Wise was second, ridden by Kirklan Cole; Blue Cloud, third, ridden by Alva Brook. The 1937 jockey champion, E. Roker, twenty wins, and second was Jockey Cleare with twelve wins.

In 1938, His Royal Highness the Duke of Windsor arrived at Montagu Park. On his right was Mr. Newell Kelly of Nassau; on his left were Captain Vyvyan Drury and Captain George Wood, who were lending their services as stewards of the track.

Snapped at Montagu Park, which opened for its fifth season in mid-January, are, left to right, Mr. Charles Austin, A.D.C. to His Excellency the Governor, the Hon. Charles Dundas, Mrs. Vanderpoel, the Hon. Mrs. Dundas, Mrs. Boatright, Commander Longdon and Mr. John Boatright. PHOTO BY TOOGOOD

The Oakes stables were the leading stable in wins, and Alfred "Uncle" Glinton won his first riding title.

Panoramic view of the race course from the club house.

In 1939, Captain Wolf became the most popular trainer. His stable consisted of twenty owners during the 1939 racing season. He saddled 270 entries, an average of 3 per race-- 34 wins, 26 seconds, and 38 thirds; Number 165 also ran, an average of 36 percent in the money (Captain Wolf of Martin Street will be in the Bahamas Racing Hall of Fame).

Panoramic view of the Race Course and
Grand Stand from the Club House.

Another product of Martin Street, Nathaniel "Tan" Bain, who rode for the Oakes stables, was second in the jockey standings with thirteen (13) wins, three seconds, and four thirds. Alfred "Uncle" Glinton was the leading jockey with sixteen wins, thirteen seconds, and seven thirds. B. Bannister, ten wins, ten seconds, and eleven thirds.

In later years, Tan Bain became the batting sensation for the St. Agnes Cricket Club.

The Nassau Guardian

NASSAU BAHAMAS SATURDAY JANUARY 6 1940

HORSE RACING

MONTAGU PARK OPENS FRIDAY

Another horse racing season will be inaugurated at Montagu Park next Friday with a programme of seven races beginning at 2.30 p.m. Many of last year's popular favourites will face the barrier again and enough new blood will be there to increase the uncertainty of the opening day results as over 100 horses are registered of which about 25 are newcomers.

The organisation has been considerably changed with Mr. Newell Kelly as Secretary replacing Mr. Stanley Marsh (who is now secretary of the Bahamas Country Club). Mr. Kelly is also taking over the thankless task of starting in place of Mr. Kirtland Cole.

A very unusual feature, which has received considerable publicity abroad as something new in racing, is the selection of a woman as handicapper. Mrs. R. K. Moore, the well-known local horsewoman who loves nothing better than to match strides or pole strokes with masculine opponents and who has always supervised the training and handling of her own stable, has undertaken this onerous duty.

A full Board of Stewards has not been named but the Hon. A. F. Adderley and Mr. A. E. J. Dupuch are former horse owners who will serve and the Hon. Capt. K. B. Meade and Mr. Harry P. Sands have also been named.

In response to requests the pari-mutuel will restore win, place and show betting as previous to last year and the daily double and quinella will be continued.

Horse owners are meeting at 4 o'clock tomorrow afternoon for a preliminary discussion and the programme for Friday will be arranged at a second meeting on Monday evening, both at the Montagu Interests office.

1940. Mrs. Agnes Moore, racing Secretary, and Handicapper. Was she the first in the world?

In 1940, racing history at Montagu Park! A very unusual feature, which had received considerable publicity abroad as something new in racing, was the selection of a woman as handicapper. Mrs. R. K. Moore, the well-known local horse woman who loves nothing better than to match strides or polo strokes with masculine opponents and who has always supervised the training and handling of her own stable, has undertaken this onerous duty (congratulations, Mrs. Moore).

NASSAU'S FIRST SWEEPSTAKE

A scene at Hobby Horse Hall on March 7, 1941, when the Duchess of Windsor drew the winning tickets in the sweepstake organized by the War Materials Committee. Left to right: The Duke of Windsor, the billiard-bald pate of Mr. Etienne Dupuch, Chairman of the Committee is seen just behind the Duke's head, the Duchess; Miss Sylvia Johnson, Secretary of the Committee, Capt. John Holmes, then a member of the Board of Works staff who built the drum for the tickets, and the Hon. Godfrey Higgs, a member of the Committee. Standing behind Miss Johnson is the late Mrs. Eugene Dupuch (Gladys Black) who was Assistant Secretary of the Committee. (See story on sweepstakes above).
— *Toogood Studio.*

At scene at Hobby Horse Hall on March 7, 1941, when the Duchess of Windsor drew the winning tickets in the sweepstake organized by the War Materials Committee. Left to right: The Duke of Windsor, the billard-bald pate of Mr. Etienne Dupuch, Chairman of the Committee is seen just behind the Duke's head, the Duchess; Miss Sylvia Johnson, Secretary of the Committee, Capt. John Holmes, then a member of the Board of Works staff who built the drum for the tickets, and the Hon. Godfrey Higgs, a member of the Committee. Standing behind Miss Johnson is the late Mrs. Eugene Dupuch (Gladys Black) who was Assistant Secretary of the Committee. (See story on sweepstakes above).

--Toogood Studio.

It was noted that Sir Harry Oakes started the construction of Oakes Airport but it was completed by American and English engineers of Pleasantville Construction Co.

The sophiscated cultural Bahamian gentleman is seen in the early days of the construction of the Oakes Airport receiving their weeks pay in most orderly manner and cultural fashion. 99.9% of each gentleman is wearing his "fedora hat" that was a part of the men of the Bahamas culture! And now it is lost!

For the first time, Pick The Winners contest was introduced to the racing fans. This exotic betting consist of selecting six winners in six consecutive races. In today's racing it is known to be the Pick Six Wager.

Two competitors succeeded in turning in their tickets naming six winners. They are Samuel Farrington, East St. South and C. H.

Forbes, Bain Town. They shared first prize money of eight pounds (to this day Bahamians are noted to be good handicappers). Would it be fair to say that Montagu Park Racetrack was the first to implement the Pick Six in horse racing in this region?

Forty-two years later, in 1982, the Pick Six Jackpot was innovated at Hialeah Park in Miami, Florida, on January 25, 1982. A winner collected $382,344.80. Another first for the historical Hobby Horse Hall (Montagu Park Racetrack).

N.J. French's "coronation" led from the start. Jockey A. Glinton

CORONATION WINS KENT CUP

Quinella and Daily Double Pay Big Odds

Mr. Jas French's Coronation won the Duke of Kent's Cup race at Montagu Park today. The cup was presented to Mr. French by Lady Oakes.

Both the Daily Double and the Quinella paid big odds today. Only four people held the Quinella: Mrs. A. B. Ford, Miss Beatrice Miller, Mr. Harcourt Carter and Mr. Mines who is employed at Mr. W. H. Sands' shop.

Mr. Mines wanted his money in cash. The others were satisfied to take cheques signed by Mr. Murphy. Last week £4,200 passed through the Parimutuel. This week the figure was £3,700.

Following are the results of today's races at Montagu Park:—

First Race — Four Furlongs — 56 1.5

1. Basil Smith's Italian Navy, Pratt 93 — 31/6, 23/6, 10/-. By a half length.
2. Empire Stables Waspite, Major 96 — 26.9, 14/-. By one length.
3. Gene Dillett's Top Row, Jones 99 — 8.9. By a head.

Second Race — Five Furlongs — 1.09 1.5

1. K. V. A. Rodgers' Branwen, Clinton 100 — 14/-, 9/3, 8/3. By one length.
2. H. G. Christie's Sun Charmer, Bannister 96 — 17/6, 10.9. By one length.
3. T. C. Johnson's Stables Rum Raisin, Davis 96 — 7.9. By one length.

Third Race — Four Furlongs — 56 1.5

1. T. G. Johnson's Stables Chocolate, Edgecombe 94 — 70/3, 26/3, 10/-. By one length.
2. T. G. Johnson's Stables Lady Carol, Penn 96 — 15.6, 13.3. By one length.
3. Empire Stables Pleasant, Rolfe 100 — 12/-. By a half length.

Daily Double

Branwen in the 2nd Race and Chocolate in the 3rd Race — £60, 12, 0.

Fourth Race — Five Furlongs — 1.07 1.5

1. Arrindale Griffiths' Venus, Clinton 104 — 19.9, 7/-, 6/6. By one length.
2. Gladstone Adderley's Renardo, Knowles 100 — 6.9, 8/-. By one length.
3. G. C. Cash's Dimple, J. Davis 100 — 10/3. By one length.

Fifth Race — One Mile — 1.54

Duke of Kent's Cup

1. N. J. French's Coronation, Clinton 100 — 10/6, 6/-, 5/3. By five lengths.
2. H. G. Christie's Capetown, Bannister 100 — 6/3, 5/3. By one length.
3. W. G. Cash's Ace, Knowles 102 — 5/3. By four lengths.

Sixth Race — Four Furlongs — .59

1. Francis Smith's Disaster, Pratt 99 — 10/9, 9.9, 7.3. By four lengths.
2. Blanche Higgs' Wait-A-While, E. Bowe 95 — 33/-, 8.9. By one length.
3. Allen Robertson's Last Chance Jones 95 — 6/6. By one length.

Seventh Race — One Mile — 1.57 1.5

1. Smith Stables No Heel, E. Bowe 94 — 24½/-, 63/9, 24/3. By three lengths.
2. Albert E. Lloyd's Three Daggers, Forbes 96 — 78/6, 51/3. By three lengths.
3. D. Munnings' Empire, Bannister 100 — 8/9. By one length.

Quinella

No Heel and Empire in the seventh race — £117, 12, 3.

Greek Fund Raffle

A Frigidaire is being offered as first prize in a raffle being sponsored by the Greek War Fund Committee. Tickets, priced at 4/-, each, will be on sale tomorrow at the Royal Bank of Canada and a list of individual vendors will appear in the Press later.

FRIDAY
MARCH
1941

N.J. French's "coronation" All alone at the finish line.

In 1941, N. J. French's Coronation and the Honorable Oswald Bancroft's Muse were the two top horses in 1941. Muse won the Cunard White Star Cup race after defeating Coronation in a match race earlier in the first race. In February 1941, N. J. French was seen receiving the most coveted trophy from Lady Eunice Oakes. Coronation was ridden by Alfred "Uncle" Glinton and trained by Captain Wolf.

Lady Eunice Oakes presents the winning trophy to Mr. N. J. French.

Alfred "Uncle" Glinton won his fourth riding title, and in second place, Harcourt "Cordy" Bastian. In future years, Harcourt became general manager of the racing facility, Hobby Horse Hall.

Montagu Park closed after the 1941 season, and with the escalation of World War II, the track remained closed for several years. Alfred "Uncle" Glinton went to Bermuda to ride.

TODAY'S RESULTS AT MONTAGU PARK

Eighth Season Has Brilliant Closing Day

The closing day at Montagu Park attracted a large and enthusiastic crowd. The weather was fine and the racing was good. Mr. Murphy recruited his friend. Mr. H. N. Kelly, to start the races and Mr. Kelly was master at the tape as he was during the time he was Secretary and Starter at the track. The starts were fast and good but the track was slow today, and so all the recorded times were behind average.

Mr. John Bastian's "Maybe" (Felix Bowe trainer, Major jockey) won the fifth race to take the Gentles' Cup. Mr. Bastian was not present for the presentation and so the cup was received by Trainer Bowe from Mrs. R. W. Taylor.

A curious thing happened in the last race of the season. Renardo, restless as usual, was prancing around. Accidentally his nose struck the tape, sprung the lever, started the race. All the horses happened to be in line and it proved to be one of the best starts of the season.

Following are the day's results:

First Race — Four Furlongs
.57 1/5
1. T. G. Johnson's Stables Chocolate, Edgecombe 90. By half length. 30/6, 13/6, 11/-.
2. Mrs. George Murphy's Chance, C. Rolle 98. By half length. 21/3, 14/9.
3. A. Griffith's Crusader, C. Bowe 100. By half length. 18/3.

Second Race — Five Furlongs
1.10 3/5
1. K. V. Rodgers' Branwen, Clinton 100. By a length. 17/6, 10/-, 8/6.
2. Mrs. George Murphy's Hurricane, Major 90. By a length. 75/-, 21/6.
3. E. G. Mitchell's Gammon, Knowles 100. By a length. 14/6.

Third Race — Five Furlongs
1.13 1/5
1. Francis Smith's Miss Calamity, Major 95. By two lengths. 13/9, 8/3, 6/6.
2. Mrs. Thomas Dean's Blue Bell, Pratt 98. By a length. 10/6, 9/-.
3. Reuben Darville's Nelson, Dean 100. By half a length. 7/6.

Daily Double
Branwen in the second race and Miss Calamity in third race — £5 6 3.

Fourth Race — Five Furlongs
1.11
1. T. G. Johnson Stables' Pepperpot, Davis 93. By a nose. 40/9, 28/3, 14/-.
2. Mrs. A. B. Malcolm's Lady Ann, Knowles 102. By two lengths. 8/6, 7/-.
3. D. Munnings' Empire, Banister 98. By a length. 10/3.
Dean on No Heel was thrown soon after the start. He was not injured.

Fifth Race — Four Furlongs
1.00
(Gentles Cup Race For Maidens)
1. John Bastian's Maybe, Major 106. By five lengths. 7/-, 6/3, 6/3.
2. Ivan R. Hall's Water Knight, Edgecombe 90. By a nose. 14/-, 8/9.
3. Harold King's Maybelle, Pratt 90. By 2 lengths. 11/3.

Sixth Race — Four Furlongs
.55 4/5
1. A. B. Malcolm's Dixiana, Jones 98. By a length. 18/3, 6/6, 6/6.
2. Alice Lightbourn's Pat Casey, Clinton 102. By a length. 5/6, 5/9.
3. L. A. Bowe and Fred Deal's Brave Boy, C. Bowe 104. By a half length. 9/9.
The Starter fined Clinton 20/- for trying to get a flying start.

Seventh Race — One Mile
1.54 4/5
1. H. G. Christie's Robert Bruce, Bannister 106. By a length. 11/6, 6/6, 6/6.
2. Gladstone Adderley's Renardo, T. Knowles 100. By half length. 9/-, 8/-.
3. E. Munnings' Bitter Spice, Jones 104. By a length. 10/6.
The Quinella — Robert Bruce and Renardo — paid £2. 2. 3.

Noted horse owners, trainers, jockeys during Montagu Park racing era were the following:

Mr. and Mrs. A. F. Adderley	Pyfrom Bros.
Mr. R. W. Turnquest	Munnings Stables
Sir Oswald Bancroft, chief justice of the Bahamas	S. J. Moses
Sir and Lady Etienne Dupuch	Paul Meeres
Mrs. A. K. Moore	Mrs. R. K. Moore
L. A. Bowe	W. H. Sands and Mr. A. K. Cole
H. Burnside	Lady Eunice Oakes
Mr. Claridge	Mr. Maury Roberts
Bahamian Club	A. B. Malcolm
H. N. Kelly	H. G. Christie
Alva Brooke	N. J. French
Basil North	Dr. K. V. A. Rodgers
Jean Dillett	Mr. Arrindale Griffith
Albert Lloyd	H. N. Chipman
Felix Johnson	Allan Roberts
Drexel Stables	F. Smith
Mr. Damianos	R. Bethell
W. G. Cash	L. Lightbourn

Trainers	Jockeys
Capt. Wolf	Alfred "Uncle" Glinton
J. Maura	Harcourt "Cordy" Bastian
Fred Marshall	Rupert Jenoure
Mackie	E. Rolle
Albert Lloyd	Dan Mackey
Cash	Dangie Love
McPhee	B. Bannister
Taylor	Harry Griffith
Lowe	"Mopy" Armbrister
Strachan	Roy Glass
S. N. Smith	Wellington Ferguson
Morley	Knowles
McGregor	Walkes
H. Smith	C. Brennen
Love	Roker
Taylor	King

Captain Red and Black Polo Team | Arnold K. Cole; Kingsbury Moore; John Sears; Jimmy Finch | 21, August 1931

Photo tribute to the Bahamas Polo Association
Ceremony at Clifford Park 1942.

The Duchess is presenting the Sir Bede Clifford Polo Cup to Capt.
Bill Pyfrom | Clifford Park - Nassau | 16, Dec. 1940
Standing left to right: Sir Harry Oakes; John F. McCarthy; Capt.
Woods; The Duchess of Windsor; The Duke of Windsor

The Lady Williams-Taylor Polo Cup Presented by the Duchess of Windsor to Capt. A.B. Malcolm of the Cannons Clifford Park - Nassau | 26, February 1942 | Refere: Hon. A.K. Cole | Umpire Major Hays Cannons Team - A.B. Malcolm; Allan Roberts; Will Pyfrom

The Blackhawks & The Pistols playing for the Sir Bede Clifford
Polo Cup | Clifford Park - Nassau | 6, December 1940
Back Row - let to right - J. Garfunkel; L. Lightbourn; A. Brooks |
Front Row - left to right - Capt. Meade; A.B. Malcolm; K. Cole

Polo Match between The Black Hawks & The Pistols playing for the
Sir Bede Clifford Cup | Clifford Park - Nassau | 6, December 1940
Standing on platform in white fur coat is Lady Oakes
& looking back is the Duchess of Windsor
In front from left to right - John McCarthy; Sir
Harry Oakes; The Duke of Windsor

In 1946, the Bethell brothers (Charles, Philip, Peter, and John) leased Montagu Park Racetrack from the Bahamas government and renamed it Hobby Horse Hall. The Bethells owned extensive liquor business, cinemas, and choice real estate in the Bahamas.

Postwar operations, the Bethells brought in horses from the Out Islands, namely Long Island, Exuma, Cat Island, and Eleuthera. As they will admit, anything with four legs that resembled a horse, a matter that was sometimes hard to ascertain!

The native horses, for most of their lives, were fed on *jumbey*, once grown in the Bahamas for cattle feed. This bush has the unfortunate propensity for making the horses lose their hair, so most of them arrived with very shaggy-looking manes and tails.

Correct feeding, continuous grooming, and proper care under the direction of Canadian-born trainer, Mr. Al Watt, soon changed wild and unkempt ponies into sleek and powerful racers.

A jockey training school was established and was made available for the young students of the art of being able to ride in races. Mr. Roker was named jockey master, and discipline was his motto!

They may not become an expert like legendary Isaacs Murphy, Willie Simms, Jimmy Winkfield, Eddie Acaro, Willie Shoemaker, Bill Hartack, Sir Gordon Richards, or our very own Gary Bain, but they were very enthusiastic about becoming a jockey.

It was told that a friend of one of the jockey student asked to attend the jockey school, and after the first day of disciplinary training, he told his friend it was too much discipline for him, so he never returned. Later it was discovered that the youngster was sent to the Boys Industrial School (sad story).

Hobby Horse Hall

(Montagu Park Racing Association Ltd.)

THE FIRST POST-WAR

RACING SEASON

WILL COMMENCE

ON

Friday, January 3rd, 1947

FIRST RACE 2.30 P.M.

PARI-MUTUEL BETTING UNDER GOVERNMENT SUPERVISION

Admission to Track and Grandstand 8/-

Admission to Club House for Guests
of Members of Jockey Club 12/- extra

N.B. Members of Jockey Club must pay Track Admission

The First Postwar Racing Season

On January 3, 1947, the Bahamians welcomed the return of horse racing in the colony, but after a few race meets, bad rumors started to spread that the races were fixed. Management realized they were partly to blame for the rumors as 99 percent of the horses listed in the racing program were owned by Hobby Horse Hall, which operated the racetrack. The Bethell brothers immediately disbursed the racehorses to private ownership, and horse racing continued with great success.

The good Old Days

Easter Monday at Hobby Horse Hall.

Start of the Gentlemen's Race 1947 Hobby Horse Hall

A.B. Malcolm's Atop "SMOKEY" Winner of the Gentlemen's Race. Unidentified Groom.

HOBBY HORSE HALL

PROGRAMME FOR FRIDAY'S RACES

First Race—Four Furlongs
1. Touche—95.
2. Sitting Bull—85.
3. Skipper—85.
4. Scatter Brain—100.
5. Sadie Green—100.
6. Daisy Mae—90.
7. Jean Lafitte—100.
8. 7 Up—90.
9. Phantom—95.

Second Race—Five Furlongs
(First half Daily Double)
1. Eggie—110.
2. Patch Work—90.
3. Boo Boo—95.
4. O'Kelly—90.
5. Three Feathers—95.
6. Jubilee—90.
7. Glamor Gal—85.
8. Zev—95.

Third Race—Five Furlongs
(Second half Daily Double)
1. Smokey—135.
2. Johanna—90.
3. Banner—95.
4. Spit Fire—100.
5. Highland Queen—85.
6. Princess Montagu—105.
7. Soldier's Farewell—95.
8. Sweetie Pie—95.
9. Henry O (Mr. Frisky)—95.

Fourth Race—One Mile
1. Hey You—105.
2. Texas (Bucaneer)—85.
3. Rogue—95.
4. Gaucho—95.
5. Red Jac—95.
6. Bonnie Laddie—95.
7. Glamor Boy—85.
8. King Copper—95.

Fifth Race—Five Furlongs
(Quinella)
1. Lady Eunice—95.
2. Rebel—90.
3. Champagne—85.
4. Montana—90.
5. Mrs. O'Grady—95.
6. Van Guard—100.
7. The Brat (Amber)—95.
8. Lightning—100.

Sixth Race—Five Furlongs
1. Rob Roy—90.
2. Vixen—85.
3. Saracen—95.
4. Bacardi—90.
5. Henry Morgan—95.
6. Serenade—95.
7. Dive Bomber—100.
8. Pirate's Gold—100.

Seventh Race—Four Furlongs
(Quinella)
1. Mid Way—85.
2. Judy—95.
3. Jack Pot—105.
4. Hurricane—95.
5. Muddy Water—95.
6. Beau Geste—100.
7. Lucky Strike—85.
8. Bad Raccoon—95.
9. Swamp Fire—95.

Nostalgia Moments

Sir Etienne and Lady Dupuch out for their morning ride. The only promise that Lady Dupuch, a keen horsewoman, exacted from her husband before marriage was that when she came to The Bahamas from her home in Spangler, Pennsylvania, she would always have a horse. She was 66 years old when she entered her last equestrian event. She and her horse, both the oldest in the show, took first prize for Equitation.

GUESS - REVIEW OF THE RACES

INTERESTING PROGRAMME AT HOBBY HORSE HALL

By "JONAH".

Once again the handicapper at Hobby Horse Hall has contrived to provide an interesting programme so that the betting public are furnished their brains and exercising their brains for the answer to the dual old puzzle. Find the two magical numbers which will pay off in the Daily Double and the Quinella.

In the first race it is interesting to note that Skipper who last ran Friday carrying 100-lbs, is now reduced to 75lbs, and that 7-Up, who came second in the same race with 86-lbs, runs to-morrow over the same distance carrying 81-lbs. Poker Face, who ran behind 7-Up carrying 82, runs to-morrow with 80. Then we find that Theme Song, carrying 90 over the Four Furlongs in the third meet, took the race from 3-Up and Skipper, and that Sadie Green, carrying 90 in the first meet, beat 7-Up, Skipper, Poker Face, and Phantom. In that race Phantom ran 75/60, carrying 95.

My guess is that 7-Up, Sadie Green, and Theme Song have a chance of coming in the money.

The first half of the Double gives Midway, who over was carrying 90 over the same distance last meet, as extra four furlong. Red Raccoon, for second, carrying 90. Some of the others have a 100 over, say the way.

It seems to me that Queen of the Bird Baracuda, and Paddy should make a race of it between them.

In the Second Half, Raphaelita is quite unknown to me. Three Feathers has beaten Eggie and Dive Bomb over Five Furlongs. Eggie ran first over Four Furlongs, carrying 90. Orphan, carrying 95, beat Baracuda, and Champagne over the same distance. Tipperary has a thing place to its credit.

Here I would say that Orphan, Baracuda, and Champagne have that reasonably good investment.

In the Six Furlong, fifth race I like Texas, Split Face, and Highland Queen. The latter came home last Friday and paid a fair race but that was over Four Furlongs. Split Face ran a good race in the same meet over the Five Furlongs. Texas also ran second over that and Texas has been a favourite by a short head from time to time.

As will soon as it is known you never know how much either of them can gain out of Bitter Wood can bring it off carrying 103-lbs, then the conclusion that at least one of the horses will be amply justified. Dapper Dan took the second half of the Double last Raccoon at Midway. As Harry ran last out over Two races has been the first, Dapper Dan came over the Four Furlongs. Her luck has over to win. My guess over the Quinella here are in another Bitter Wood. My guess to the same three horses as the race from Mr. Harry as Bitter Wood.

In the Quinella, the six races good, or if I am not mistaken so far in to a four race, for once a race. Phantom was still on the race. In this contest.

al Van Guard, the third Rebel and Johnson have been fast in the money. Bar war, Lightning, and O'Reilly ought not to be too far out of it.

In the last race The Brat, Henry Mungo, and Patch Work would help to make a race of it. My Time may also be worth watching.

The following is the programme for to-morrow's races:—

First Race—Four Furlongs

1. Sadie Green—90.
2. Phantom—94.
3. Skipper—75.
4. Jean Lafitte—84.
5. Poker Face—80.
6. Scatter Brain—102.
7. 7-Up—81.
8. Theme Song—78.
9. Capt. Kidd—110.

Second Race—Four Furlongs (First half Daily Double)

1. Paddy—94.
2. Jody—90.
3. Tourbo—90.
4. Jack Pot—90.
5. Swamp Fire—90.
6. Glamor Gal—106.
7. Mid Water—90.
8. Daisy Mae—85.
9. Red Raccoon—190.

Third Race—Four Furlongs (Second half Daily Double)

1. Raphael
2. Dive Bomber—
3. Tipperary—
4. Champagne—100.
5. Saracen—90.
6. Raphaelita—90.
7. Orphan—105.
8. Three Feathers—105.

Fourth Race—Six Furlongs

1. Highland Queen—105.
2. Glamor Boy—95.
3. Montana—95.
4. Red Jac—95.
5. Mauve—95.
6. Dream E—95.
7. Split Face—105.
8. Texas (Hinesworth)—95.

Fifth Race—Four Furlongs

1. Rogue—100.
2. Snowy—120.
3. Bill—120.
4. Vacarius—95.
5. Bitter Wood—110.
6. Ionatha—95.
7. Er Barry—115.
8. Boy Van—95.
9. Dapper Dan—105.

Sixth Race—Four Furlongs (Quinella)

Jackie—90.
Lightning—90.
Rebel—95.
Van Guard—107.
Rebel—
O'Reilly—90.
Mr. Burr (Black Beauty)—100.

Seventh Race—Four Furlongs

1. The Brat
2. Sensation—90.
3. Two Step (Arawak)—95.
4. Diamond Jack—
5. Patch Work—95.
6. My Time—90.
7. Henry Mungo—95.
8. My Luck—90.
9. Alex Barracuda—

THE HIGH COST OF PRICE SECURITY

By H. G. L. STRANGE
Former Economic Department

ARRIVALS

By P.A.A. from yesterday.
Howard Pine, Robert Noyes, Arthur Jones, Earl Munn, Joseph

Panoramic view of the Race Course and
Grand Stand from the Club House.

ENTRIES IN THE NEXT RACE are walked around the paddock while spectators in the Jockey Club take a final look at their selections before crossing to the pari-mutuel windows to place their bets. Modern American Tote equipment is used and the pari-mutuel betting is under Government supervision.–Colyn Rees

Spectators stroll from the Jockey Club to the Paddock to give the horses a final check before the signal for closing pari-mutuel windows.

Sir Victor Sassoon, noted horseman and banker, arrived in the Bahamas for the first time in 1947 and fell in love with the country. He was impressed with the stability and potential growth for the country and its wonderful people that he transferred his Sassoon banking empire to the Bahamas. It is also interesting to note that twenty-two years later, Mr. Paul Adderley, former attorney general and former minister of education, addressed a Unicom meeting and told the members to welcome foreign investors and make them Bahamians (a very interesting comment for today's Bahamas––some foresight).

April 8, 1947, two thousand additional Bahamian farmworkers were recruited for work in Florida.

Buster Johnson, champion jockey for 1947––twenty-four wins and eighteen seconds.

Henry Cleare in second place with twenty-two wins and twenty-four seconds.

Philip Major, twelve wins and twenty seconds, in third.

Photo by Stanley Toogood, A.R.P.S.
David Farrar, British movie star, gallops along the beach
astride "Smokey" during a vacation at Nassau.

HOBBY HORSE HALL

PROGRAMME FOR FRIDAY'S RACES

First Race—Five Furlongs
1. Jean Lafitte—80.
2. Glamor Gal—90.
3. Muddy Water—95.
4. Bacardi—99.
5. Vixen—95.
6. Anne Bonney—95.
7. Lucky Strike—95.
8. Half and Half—95.
9. Patch Work—100.

Second Race—Four Furlongs
(First half Daily Double)
1. Swamp Fire—88.
2. Henry Morgan—90.
3. Sun Beam—90.
4. Dynamite—85.
5. Dive Bomber—110.
6. Jack Pot—90.
7. Rob Roy—95.
8. Beau Geste—105.

(Second half Daily Double)
Gentlemen's Race
Third Race—Six Furlongs
1. Highland Queen—Mr. H. Porrelli.
2. Texas (Horsurer)—Mr. B. Butler.
3. Red Jac—Mr. A. K. Cole.
4. Jubilee—Mr. R. Maura.
5. Smokey—Mr. A. B. Malcolm.
6. Montana—Mr. P. Bethell.
7. Bonnie Laddie—Mr. A. Johanson.
8. Glamor Boy—Mr. A. L. Watt.

Fourth Race—Four Furlongs
1. Paddy—90.
2. Mrs. O'Grady—105.
3. Lady Ennire—85.
4. The Brat (Amber)—95.
5. Serenade—90.
6. Flicker—90.
7. Saragon—85.
8. Lightning—100.
9. Champagne—97.

Fifth Race—Six Furlongs
(Quinella)
1. Girlie—110.
2. Hey You—105.
3. Gaucho—90.
4. Yankee—90.
5. Rogue—95.
6. Princess Montagu—91.
7. Sweetie Pie—85.
8. Trapper Dan—107.
9. Spit Fire—85.

Sixth Race—Four Furlongs
1. Phantom—95.
2. 7-Up—90.
3. Theme Song—85.
4. Mid Way—95.
5. Skipper—94.
6. Fincastle—80.
7. Tourke—95.
8. Daisy Mae—90.
9. Spike Green—105.

Seventh Race—Five Furlongs
(Quinella)
1. Ripple—90.
2. Johanna—90.
3. Pirate's Gold—95.
4. Zev—100.
5. O'Kelly—85.
6. Van Guard—90.
7. Three Feathers—90.
8. Soldier's Farewell—105.
9. Boo Boo—95.

Photographed at Hobby Horse Hall with a group of young jockey's were, left to right, Miss Edith Gresham, Mr. Bert Bertram, Miss Lilliam Gish, and Mr. Bill Kester of the Bahamas Playhouse. Below spectators take a last look at the horses in the paddock before the race.

During the summer of 1948, Hobby Horse Hall management contacted Mr. Willis "Bill" Minns of Poitier Lane South off East Bay Street to design and build an electric starting gate. In the early years, a sort of Heath Robinson contraption of pulleys and ropes were used as a starting tape.

The Bahamas first electrical starting gate at Hobby Horse Hall. Built by a Bahamian,

Photo by Frederic Moure

Jockeys weigh in.

L. R the late Bernie Nichols, Sammie Saunders, Theophils "Mr. T." Fritz and, jockey Larrymore.

Jockey's weighing in at Hobby Horse Hall. They are as concerned with their weight as fashion models, and will go to incredible lengths to avoid extra poundage.

The Bethells operated the track for three seasons and invested tremendous sums of money into improvements, landscaping, and general maintenance, which created a diversification of jobs for carpenters, masons, electricians, plumbers, and a large number of general laborers. In addition, trainers, grooms, jockeys, stable boys, and hot walkers were given year-round employment. The natives saw this as a part of the economic growth of the Bahamas, and their chant was we have tourism contract and racetrack. Horse racing became the dominant culture of the Bahamian people.

The Earl of Carnavon owner of Hobby Horse Hall circa, 1950.

At the end of the 1949 racing season, the Bethell brothers sold the controlling stock of the Montagu Park Racing Association to the Earl of Carnarvon, son of Lord Carnarvon, who financed the expedition in the discovery of the ancient tomb of King Tut. The balance of the stock was sold to Mr. Tim Macauley of Canada. The Bethells contended that they made a lot of money during the years they operated the racetrack, and the only reason they sold the track was because on race days, the then commissioner of police failed to give them police protection.

After the 1950 racing season, the Earl of Carnarvon and Mr. Macauley sold their interests in the track to Mr. Alexis Nihon, Belgian-born and well-known Canadian industrialist who also was a winter resident of Nassau for several years.

During the summer of 1950, Mr. Nihon directed Mr. Al Watt, general manager of Hobby Horse Hall, to import English Thoroughbred horses to the Bahamas to upgrade racing and breeding.

1951 Race Season

Boxing Day Jumkanoo | A.B. Malcolm | Nassau | 1951

You'll only find one race on the card with Thoroughbreds, but you will see fast-spirited small Bahamian ponies. A picturesque tropical setting and the gathering of glamorous celebrities who attended the races at Hobby Horse Hall, the only racetrack of its kind in the world, add a fillip of excitement to the ancient sport of kings.

Ivan James

Start of the 3rd Race March 16th, 1951

Gallant Man
Texas
Lighting
Hey You
Flora
Anne Bonney
Princess Montague
Gaucho
Lady Ann

EAGER CROWDS WATCH A RACE START
AT HOBBY HORSE HALL--Colyn Rees

Sir Victor Sassoon Wins British Colonial Cup

THE NASSAU G

Sir Victor Sassoon Wins British Colonial Cup

Yesterday was even a more exciting day than usual at Hobby Horse Hall race track, and the audience were certainly thrilled when they watched Sir Victor Sassoon's horse, Nassau Eve, win by a short head the mile race and so carry off the much coveted British Colonial Cup.

Before the running of the race, the large, magnificent cup was on view in front of the Members' Stand. Many of our visitors were very much intrigued by it and had themselves photographed next to it as a souvenir.

The presentation, made by Mr. Kenneth Arnold, Manager of the British Colonial Hotel, was held on the lawn opposite the stand and everyone gathered round to listen to Sir Victor's short speech.

Sir Victor said: "I have raced in many countries all over the world, and the more I race the less I know about racing." He also added how happy he was that the winning horse bore the name Nassau Eve and that it was not the first time that his "second string" had won.

For all to see at close quarters, the gallant horse who had won the cup was brought on to the lawn by her little jockey, R. Woods, dressed in his gay racing colours.

Both amateur and professional pictures were taken of the horse, the owner and the cup, as well as a few motion picture film shots.

Once more stage and film stars were amongst the racegoers, and this time it was handsome John Loder, star and producer of "For Love or Money" which has been shown at the Bahama Playhouse this week.

Mr. and Mrs. Alexis Nihon's box was again the centre of attention, for besides Mr. Loder and Mr. Kenneth Arnold from the British Colonial, there was also Mrs. Loder, looking extremely beautiful in a bright red dress.

Betting as usual was brisk, and the Daily Double paying a dividend of £67 9 9 was very popular.

The clothes seemed to strike an even brighter note than usual, yellow being the predominant colour of the day. There were quite a few ladies in slacks and shorts and amongst the large gathering, the American Navy was well represented.

The sun shone brightly throughout the afternoon and it was not till dusk that the hundreds of cars and taxis were racing their way back along the coastal road to Nassau.

115

MOIRA KENNEDY, charming daughter of Mr. and Mrs. Allan Kennedy, who won the Ladies Race on Bigird Amoury's "Gaucho" at Montagu Park on Friday.

The racing fans were certainly thrilled when they watched Sir Victor Sassoon's horse, Nassau Eve, ridden by Ronald "Ding" Woods, win the much-coveted British Colonial Cup Race. Sir Victor said, "I have raced in many countries all over the world, and the more I race, the less I know about racing." He also added how happy he was that the winning horse bore the name Nassau Eve and that it was not the first time that his second string had won. The order of finish:

Nassau Eve	First
Queen of Clonmel	Second
Misty Eve	Third

CUP PRESENTATION

WRESTLING BOUTS AT HOBBY HORSE HALL

117

March 21, 1951

Wrestling Matches at Hobby Horse Hall. For the first time in the history of the colony, organized wrestling is being brought to Nassau.

Comedian and singer Richard Sunny Valle entertains the racing fans at Hobby Horse Hall Race Track. The late Mr. James Sweeting on the drums.

There will be four in all: two by local boys and two by foreigners. Danny Dusek versus Dan O'Conner, Prince Omar of Persia and Angelo Martinelli of Boston. Local talent Theophilus "Mighty Mouse" Fritz versus Edward G. Man Robinson. Roland Crusher Williams versus Leo "the Lion" Bowen.

HHH Registers Dead Heat in 7th

March 26, 1951
Proud Moment for Sir Harry's Jockey

PROUD MOMENT FOR SIR HARRY'S "JOCKEY"

— *Photo by Colyn Rees.*
MRS. HARRY B. SANDS is pictured above proudly holding the Richard Greene Trophy after riding "Sir Harry" to victory in the Social Ladies Race at Hobby Horse Hall on Easter Monday. Mrs. Sands was presented the Trophy by Richard Greene, popular London stage and screen star, who recently starred in the "Voice of the Turtle" at the Bahama Playhouse in Nassau

The festive race on Easter Monday was the Ladies Social Race for the Richard Greene Trophy won by Mrs. H. B. Sands riding Sir Harry from the Oakes stables and trained by Dennis Scully. Mr. Richard Greene, the well-known English film and stage actor who recently starred in *Voice of the Turtle* at the Bahama Playhouse in Nassau.

Day at the Races 1951.

L.R. Mr. Roddy Williams Mayor of Bermuda with Mr. Jack Tucker and Mr. William Frith also of Bermuda.

LEONARD KNOWLES receiving the cup he won in the Gentlemen's Race at Hobby Horse Hall on Friday. It was presented by Mrs. Harry B. Sands who won the Ladies Race the previous Friday. Also in the picture is Ray Milland, famed movie star who took the leading role in "Lost Weekend".

Day At The Races

Above Elizabeth Arden (Graham) at Hobby Horse Hall Race Track guest of Mr. E. P. Taylor the noted stable owner of Toronto Canada and the Lyford Cay Development here in the Bahamas. It is interesting to note that Mrs. Graham also race horses, and in 1947 Mrs. Grahams Jet Pilot won the most prestigious Horse Race in the U.S.A the Kentucky Derby, and seventeen years later Mr. E.P. Taylor's horse "Northern Dancer" won the 1964 Kentucky Derby and also Americas most loved race horse "Sea Biscuit" trainer Tom Smith was Jet Pilots.

Mr. Jeffery Lynn with Mrs. Martis Manulis
photograph between Races.

Mr. Alexis Nihon, president and owner of Hobby
Horse Hall with Mr. Everette Horton.

GLORIA DE HAVEN and her husband enjoyed the races at Nassau's unique track during their honeymoon.--Colyn Rees

The grounds have been sartorially conscious this season at Hobby Horse Hall. Many important fashion editors have been seen taking pictures during the race meetings. Noticeable were Esquire of New York and Man and His Clothes of London. The local press have been there every week writing society columns.

Mr. and Mrs. Carilse photographed between races

A view of the Club House taken from the odds board. Below, getting away to a good start. The track operates a modern photo-finish camera from the tower opposite the finish line, from which this photograph was taken.

A busy scene in the attractively-landscaped grounds of the Club stand at Hobby Horse Hall, looking from the parimutuel windows towards the paddock.

BAHAMIAN RACE HORSES parade for the spectators in the paddock before a race at Hobby Horse Hall. Young jockeys make up in enthusiasm whatever they may lack in professional skill as equestrians.

Photos by Lew Phillips

Spectators move from the Paddock to the betting windows and the clubhouse. Pari-mutuel betting is under government supervision and American totalisator machines are in operation at the track. In addition there is an automatic starting gate and photo finish equipment.

AT HOBBY HORSE HALL MEET –– Mr. and Mrs. Gregg Juarez, whose recent wedding received wide publicity locally and abroad, attended Hobby Horse Hall's "sport of kings," on Friday. Mrs. Juarez is the former Miss Fredericka Sigrist of Prospect Ridge, Nassau.

A Day at the Races

Hobby Horse Hall

The Bethel Brothers Charlie, John, Philip and Peter is seen Hobb Nobbing with Mr. Alexis Nihon owner of Hobby Horse Hall Race Track.

1952

THE NASSAU GUARDIAN WEDNESDAY APRIL 2 1952

The Ladies' Race at Hobby Horse Hall on last Friday afternoon created considerable interest. Five Miami horsewomen competed against four Bahamian young ladies for the Eve Cup donated by Sir Victor Sassoon. This picture was taken after Sir Victor (seen holding Gale of Wind) had presented the beautiful trophy to Miss Carolyn Austin, of Miami, the proud winner of the trophy.—Photo by June Studio.

The Ladies' Race at Hobby Horse Hall on last Friday afternoon created considerable interest. Five Miami horsewomen competed against four Bahamian young ladies for the Eve Cup donated by Sir Victor Sassoon. This picture was taken after Sir Victor (seen holding Gale of Wind) had presented the beautiful trophy to Miss Carolyn Austin, of Miami, the proud winner of the trophy. Photo by June Studio.

Miami and Nassau were well represented in the Ladies Race at Hobby Horse Hall, when Carolyn Austin of Miami rode Gale of Wind into first place to capture the prestigious Eve Cup donated by Sir Victor Sassoon. Sheila Pritchard of Nassau rode Pepsi into second position. Another American, Eleanor Schwartz of Miami, took third.

IMI AND NASSAU were well represented in the Ladies Race at Hobby Horse Hall
.orday when Carolyn Austin of Miami rode Gale of Wind into first place to cap-
the Eve Cup, donated and presented by Sir Victor Sassoon. Sheila Pritchard of
sau rode Pepsi into second position. Another Miamian, Eleanor Schwartz, took third.
Miamians, who were guests at the British Colonial Hotel, are leaving Nassau tomor-
by the Nuevo Dominicano. From left to right: Jacqueline Chase, Cecile Kirby,
icia Close, Eleanor Schwartz, Barbara Watt, Carol Johnson, Sheila Pritchard, and
ra Kennedy. With cup in front is winner Carolyn Austin. (See story page 3).
— *Tribune Photo.*

NASSAU BAHAMAS WEDNESDAY FEBRUARY 27 1952

A large crowd of enthusiastic racing fans look on as Mr. Donald Delahey presents the Prince George Hotel Champagne Cup to Mr. H. Bastian, trainer of Mr. R. Frost's Mint Julep who won the race at Hobby Horse Hall on Friday afternoon.

February 2, 1952

Mint Julep, owned by Mr. R. Pratt, ran away with the Prince George Champagne Cup Friday at Hobby Horse Hall. The presentation was made by Mr. Donald Delahey to the trainer, Harcourt Bastian.

Tuesday April 15, 1952
Hobby Horse Hall Noted Racing Fan, Eighty Years Old
The Real King of John Canoe

JOSHUA SYMONETTE, who led the Johnnie Canoe parade in the "Market" for a full generation, took unto himself a wife in a ceremony performed at the Transfiguration Baptist Church by the Rev. C. H. Thompson yesterday afternoon. "Josh" says he has lost count of his age. He may be 80, more or less. But he had all the glamour of a young "buck" for his wedding day. Every year Josh organizes a bicycle race round the island, he never wins, but he always finishes the course. He says he is determined to win this race with matrimony which he accepts as a challenge to his 80 years.
— *Tribune Photo.*

Joshua Symonette, who led the Johnnie Canoe Parade on Bay Street for a full generation, took himself a wife in a ceremony performed at the Transfiguration Baptist Church, Farm Road and Vesey Street by the Reverend C. H. Thompson. Euphelia Cartwright was his bride, and Mr. W. P. B. Cooper was best man.

Mrs. Al Watt presented the Canada Dry Cup to Mr. Arrindale Griffith at Hobby Horse Hall yesterday after his horse "April" won the first Quinella.

Easter Monday Racing At Hobby Horse Hall...

Large Crowd Sees "April" Win Canadian Club Cup

Sparkle and Mystery made a surprise winning in the Daily Double at Hobby Horse Hall yesterday afternoon and paid a record purse for the season of £279, 8, 9. Mrs. Albert Liddy, owner of Mystery, Philip Kemp, Van Thap, Ellie Minnis, Marjory and Helen Black, were a few of the twenty-six lucky winners. Over £7,000 went into the pool for the Double, taking a considerable amount out of circulation and causing the volume of betting to slacken off for the remainder of the afternoon.

The first race, four furlongs, was won by Delilah in the very good time of 56 secs. Raggle Taggle finished second while Tarzana surprised the public by finishing third. Baba, one of the favourites, was left in the starting gates. She started but finished in ninth position.

The first mile and a quarter race run this season created a great deal of excitement when Sparkle finished in first position. Boo Boo, which has the reputation of the long distance horse on the track, finished second. Bitter Weed came in a nose ahead of Okapi and finished in third position. This race was very closely bunched throughout the first eight furlongs and it was not until the home stretch was reached that the horses started to drive.

The second half of the daily double, a mile race, was won by Mystery which was never challenged after the four-furlong post and took an easy first. Dapper Dan ran in first position for the first four furlongs but went lame and finished a quarter of a mile behind the other runners. Son O' Mine finished in second position with Lady Ann finishing third.

The fourth race was won by Gallant Man while second, third and fourth positions were a photo finish with Conya, Bravo, Champagne, and Porter finishing respectively.

The Canada Dry Cup race was won by Mr. Arrindale Griffith's April, making her first win for the season. Mrs. Al Watt presented the trophy to the owner. Second was taken by Glamour Gal, while third and fourth were taken by Yankee and Don Alicia.

The sixth race was won by Tallula Blaze coming in for the first time this season and also breaking the track record for the four furlong distance. Misty Eve, which consistently ran in the money this season, finished second. Dolly Blue finished in third position and Hustling Count came in fourth. Two of the favourites, Sam's Girl and Nassau Eve, did not run in the money.

The last quinella was won by Honey Boy in the very good time of 1 minutes 10 seconds, with All Smiles and

(Continued on page 2)

WINS
£279. 8. 9

JUBILANTLY Mr. Fan Thap displays his £279. 8. 9 winning at Hobby Horse Hall yesterday after being one of the 26 people who "hit" the Daily Double. Mr. Thap has had three other big wins this season. The first one was with numbers three and five on which he won £298. 10. 0; the second with numbers four and six which yielded him £73; the third, yesterday, with numbers nine and two.

To pick his horses Mr. Thap does not use the programme because he does not read English. He picks his horses by looking at them.

Tribune Photo.

Hobby Horse Hall: Ms. Olga Borghardt was crowned the most beautiful girl in Nassau. Mr. Errol Flynn, movie actor, was one of the judges.

Bahamas government appoint the first Racing Commission, chairman, Dr. R. W. Sawyer.

Mr. Alexis Nihon says he will sell the racetrack after the 1953 season.

Mr. and Mrs. J. F. C. Bryce, owners of the Mill River Racing stables of New York, donated the stallion Hedron to Hobby Horse Hall management to enhance the breeding in the colony.

Nihon Bans *Tribune* from Track

Tribune reporters were banned from the racetrack today when Mr. Alexis Nihon, owner of Hobby Horse Hall, told them they could not take pictures because he didn't like the pictures they took and the captions they used.

After making a scene at the track, Mr. Nihon ordered Etienne Dupuch Jr. and Bernard Dupuch to leave the grounds.

Mr. Nihon cancelled his advertising in the *Tribune* and *What to Do* magazine after the editor's comments on racing in Nassau in his column on Monday.

CHAMPAGNE CUP WINNER—British Colonial Hotel Assistant anager Paul Nash (right) congratluates owner, jockey and groom for Delilah's win in the Champagne Cup race during Friday's Hobby Horse Hall programme. Left to right, Arthur Griffith, owner of "Delilah," jockey Eddy Codet, S. Demeritte, groom, and Mr. Nash.
—(Photo by John Bethel)

Nihon Bans Tribune from Track

The *Tribune* reporters were banned from the racetrack when Mr. Alexis Nihon, owner of Hobby Horse Hall, told them they could not take pictures because he did not like the pictures they took and the captions used. After making a scene at the track, Mr. Nihon ordered Etienne Dupuch Jr. and Bernard Dupuch to leave the grounds.

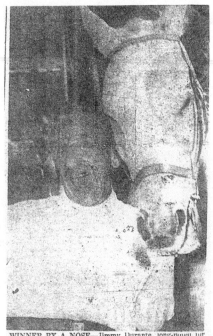

WINNER BY A NOSE—Jimmy Durante, long-noted for his ability to pick horses that lose by a nose, was back at his favourite pastime Friday at Hobby Horse Hall. Judging by Jimmie's exuberant smile, it looks as if he finally selected a winner. But, then, the horse is laughing; too.
(Guardian Picture.)

* * *

Tuesday, February 24, 1953

Racing Commission takes action against Hobby Horse Hall.

ALEXIS NIHON
. . . Inspection Thursday

Following Tuesday's Racing Commission order revoking the racecourse license, Mr. Alexis Nihon, owner of the track, said Tuesday night that he plans to have the gate in operating order by Thursday so that the commission can inspect them.

Inspection of Starting Gate smooth as silk.

Racing Commission restored HHH racing license. Mr. Nihon informed the local press that racing will resume on Friday. Miss Moira Kennedy was a proud girl after her Estrelitta won the Fort Montagu Beach Hotel Cup Race, ridden by C. Moxey and trained by Harcourt Bastian.

World famous movie actor and Oscar winner Charlton Heston and his lovely wife congratulates Miss Moria Kennedy Owner of the winning horse "Estrelita" at Hobby Horse Hall Race Track Jockey C. Moxey atop "Estrelita" trainer Harcourt "No Nonsense" Bastian looks on.

MOIRA KENNEDY, charming daughter of Mr. and Mrs. Allan Kennedy, who won the Ladies Race on Sigied Amoury's "Gaucho" at Montagu Park on Friday.

Friday, March 13, 1953

THE BRITISH COLONIAL HOTEL TROPHY went to His Jewel in the nine furlong Cup Race at Hobby Horse Hall yesterday. Mr. Reginald G. Ne'gzar, Manager of the Colonial, is pictured presenting the Hotel trophy to His Jewel's owner, Miss Viola Greenidge. On the left it seen Joseph Rolle. The jockey is A. Glinton. —*Tribune Photo.*

Ms. Viola Greenidge's His Jewel won the British Colonial Hotel nine-furlong cup race, ridden by Alfred "Uncle" Glinton and trained by Joseph "Joe Billy" Rolle.

Friday, March 27, 1953

Sheila Alvarez rides Airborne to capture Alexis Nihon Trophy.

April 10, 1953

Pulling out of the last bend Carrol Johnson on Bitter Weed
started to bear down on Captain Kidd, ridden by Barbara
Watt who held the lead at this point in the Ladies Race for
the Governors Cup yesterday. Brave Boy (Arrow) is seen
shortly after throwing Moira Kennedy. Shortly after this
Bitter Weed took the lead and held it to the finish.

MISS CARROL JOHNSON, WINNER OF THE LADIES GOV-
ERNOR'S CUP CLASSIC AT HOBBY HORSE HALL YESTERDAY.
(SEE STORY PAGE 6)   — Tribune Photo

Carol Johnson rides Bitter Weed to cup victory. Ms. Johnson is the
attractive daughter of Mr. and Mrs. Thad Johnson of Nassau.

LADIES' RACE
HER AWARD
WINNER GETS

Hobby Horse H:

As Nih

NOT ENOUGH COURAGE—When film star Arthur
Treacher presented a similar award recently, he kissed the
winner, but Colonial Secretary A. G. H. Gardner-Brown
admitted Friday he didn't have the courage to follow Mr.
Treacher's example. Mr. Gardner-Brown represented the
Governor in awarding the Governor's Cup to Miss Carol

Friday rode Basil Butler's Bitter Weed to victory over the six-furlong
course, capturing the Governor's Trophy.

Hobby Horse Hall ends 1953 season as Nihon reveals track sold. May
continue as president under new owners.

The 1953 racing season at Hobby Horse Hall closed Friday after a most interesting and exciting meet.

It was one of the most successful seasons in the history of the local racetrack.

Mr. Nihon refuses to say to whom the racetrack has been sold or how much money was involved in the transaction.

Naturally, Mr. Nihon said, "I will always be interested in the Bahamas and its people. I love Nassau."

May 1953

Dr. Raymond W. Sawyer, M.H.A.

Today's Personality

Most of Nassau enjoys a free, relaxing afternoon every Friday when the shops close down for the weekly half-holiday. But one man who will not be able to relax with the majority for several months is Dr. Raymond W. Sawyer, M.H.A., President of the Montagu Park Racing Association.

While some 2,000 racing fans play the horses and enjoy themselves at Hobby Horse Hall each Friday, Dr. Sawyer puts in his busiest day of the week.

Seldom excited, and always genial and soft-spoken to his friends and visitors to the track, he is constantly on the move, making certain everything runs smoothly and according to schedule.

Operating Hobby Horse Hall is only part of his work—he also has a dental practice to maintain.

Born in Nassau in 1905, Dr. Sawyer received his early education in England before entering the University of North Carolina and later the University of Pennsylvania, where he was graduated with a degree in dental surgery.

Following his graduation, he returned to Nassau to begin his dental practice. A year later, he married the former Ivarene Borden of Philadelphia.

During World War II, he served for two years with the Royal Canadian Dental Corps at Royal Canadian Air Force

Dr. Raymond W. Sawyer
. . . Hobby Horse Hall

stations in Ontario and Quebec.

In 1946 — two years after his discharge—he won a bye-election in the City District for the House of Assembly and has represented the area since.

With the purchase of Hobby Horse Hall from Canadian businessman, Alexis Nihon, in May, 1953, Dr. Sawyer became President of the Montagu Park Racing Association Ltd. Under his operation, the track has seen progress and improvements. One of the most important achievements has been the installation of totalisator machines for the pari-mutel betting.

Dr. R. W. Sawyer became president and managing director of Montagu Park Racing Association Ltd. and Hobby Horse Hall Racetrack in May 1953.

Born in Nassau in 1905, he received his early education in England before entering the University of North Carolina and later the University of Pennsylvania, where he graduated with a degree in dental surgery.

In 1946, he won a by-election in the city district for the House of Assembly.

147

1954

Daily Double Clicks To Tune Of £61

The 1954 racing season at Hobby Horse Hall opened with a bang Tuesday when several thousand Bahamians and visitors watched Lawrence Lightbourn's Champagne come from behind to beat the favourites by close to a length to capture the first half of the daily double.

Combined with another surprise win by L. N. Wells' Gallant Lady, the daily double clicked to the tune of £61 11 6.

The feature of the afternoon's racing — which was attended by His Excellency the Governor and Lady Ranfurly — was the Argus Handicap, which was won by Venus, owned by John Tilizos. Mr. O. W. Ray, of the O. W. Ray Corporation in New York, presented the Argus cup to Mr. Tiliacos. Some 200 sales dealers of the New York firm watched the races.

The last race was run in near darkness, as the seven-race programme, using the newly - installed ticket selling machines, came to an end. It was the first race meet at Hobby Horse Hall since Dr. R. W. Sawyer took over the ownership and management of the track.

THE WEATHER

The cool weather will continue, but a bright sunny day is expected. The fresh north-north east breeze will persist giving a ra'her choppy sea with some swells. Temperatures will be in the 60's all day with maximum of about 68 but will fall to the 40's during the night.

Race Results

First Race, Three Furlongs
Time 41 7/10 secs.
1. Mayotte 25/- 17/3 16/-
2. Shadow 30/- 17/9
3. Patsy K. 24/9

Second Race, Four Furlongs
Time 56 6/10 secs.
1. Champagne 204/6 60/- 30/3
2. Tuvlar 30/3 22/3
3. Fair Wind 54/6

Third Race, Three Furlongs
Time 38 3/10 secs.
1. Gallant Lady 69/- 30/3 20/t
2. Brave Boy 69/- 30/6
3. Don Patch 16/-
Daily Double — 4 and 1:
£61 11 3

Fourth Race, Six Furlongs
Time 1.29 secs.
1. Cheyenne 26/3 18/6 14/9
2. Recovery 69/9 30/6
3. Son O Mine 16/-

Fifth Race, Eight Furlongs
Time 1.52 2/10 secs.
1. Venus 30/9 19/3 18/3
2. Rajah 15/6 13/6
3. Glamour Gal 12/6
Quinella—1 and 4—£3 10 9

Sixth Race, Four Furlongs
Time 54 4/10 secs.
1. Yeddy (Black Label) 109/6 25/- 32/-
2. Valient 25/- 28/6
3. Rebel 40/3
Quinella—7 and 4—£4 1 0

Seventh Race, Five Furlongs
Time 1.09 secs.
1. Dotty 33/3 23/3 18/3
2. Shirley 23/3 40/9
3. Belle Star 17/6
Quinella—5 and 1—£4 13 9

VENUS WINS ARGUS CUP — Mr. John Tiliacos proudly displays the Argus Cup presented to him by Mr. O. W. Ray, left, of the O. W. Ray Corporation of New York, after Venus ran away with the Argus Handicap at Tuesday's race meet. Taking part in the presentation ceremony were Mr. Robert Lewis, President of the O. W. Ray Corporation and Dr. R. W. Sawyer, right, president of the Montagu Park Racing Association. (Guardian Picture).

Hundreds attend the opening of the beautiful Hobby Horse Hall Racetrack for the first time in the track history. Fifty totalizator ticket machines were in operation. The betters were very elated to experience the cursory effect in purchasing tickets.

February 26, 1954

Davis rides Yankee to perfect win in race for Colonial Trophy.

Mrs. Mary Armbrister, proud owner of the winning horse and trained by her husband, Mopy Armbrister, was presented with the trophy by noted stage and film star Louise Allbritton and her equally famous husband, Charles Collingwood, popular news commentator of CBS.

March 5, 1954
Three-Year-Olds Go to Post Today
In Five Hundred Pounds Cup Race

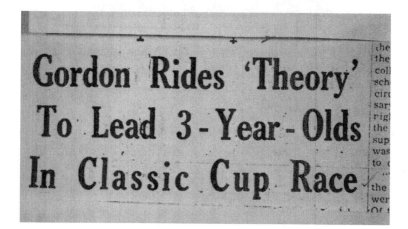

History will be made today when eight three-year-old horses contest a mile-long race for £500 purse and a handsome cup to be presented by the Racing Commission chairman to the winning pony.

Three-Year-Old Entries

(1) Theory

(4) Greystone

(2) Beware

(5) Mayotte

(3) Sabre King

(6) Tulyar

(7) Magic Moment

(8) Mark Twain

AFTER-THE-RACES drink was enjoyed by Mr. and Mrs. Charles Collingwood (she's Louise Allbriton) with their host for the afternoon Dr. R. W. Sawyer.
—Colyn Rees

After-the-races drink was enjoyed by Mr. and Mrs. Charles Collingwood (she's Louise Allbriton) with their host for the afternoon, Dr. R. W. Sawyer.

--Colyn Rees

CHAMPION THREE-YEAR-OLD—"Theory", with jockey
E. Gordon up, took his trainer's theoretical teaching and
put it to practical use Friday when he walked off with the
one-mile £400 added purse fourth race feature of Hobby
Horse Hall. By virtue of his win "Theory" was proclaimed
the champion three-year-old pony for the 1954 season and
was awarded the Racing Commission's three-foot-tall
bronze floating trophy. Picture left to right are Nigel
Jones, owner of "Theory," displaying cup; George Baker,
Chairman Racing Commission who made the presentation;
"Theory", with Gordon aboard, and proud trainer E. Mc-
Gregor.—(Picture by Colyn Rees)

Gordon Rides Theory to Lead Three-Year-Olds in Classic Cup Race

With practical demonstration, Friday afternoon, and before Hobby Horse Hall's record attendance, Mr. Nigel Jones's Theory wasted no time in proving his right to be champion three-year-old of 1954. The newly appointed Racing Commission chairman, Mr. George Baker, congratulated Mr. Jones and Theory's jockey, Edward Gordon, and trainer, E. "Biddy" McGregory. Also in attendance were Mr. William C. Langley, member of the State of New York Race Commission, and his son-in-law, Mr. Walter Fletcher, vice president of Aqueduct Racetrack Commission, as guests of Dr. R. W. Sawyer.

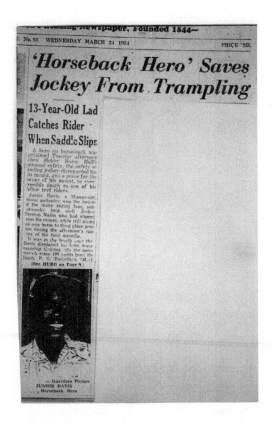

—Founded 1844—

No. 93 WEDNESDAY MARCH 24 1954   PRICE 3D.

'Horseback Hero' Saves Jockey From Trampling

13-Year-Old Lad Catches Rider When Saddle Slips

A hero on horseback was acclaimed Tuesday afternoon when Hobby Horse Hall's Personal Safety, the safety of leading jockey disregarded his mount, and a purse for the owner of his mount, to avert possible death to one of his fellow turf riders.

Junior Davis, a 13-year-old, whose gallantry won the hearts of the many racing fans, sensationally held aloft Jockey Preston Nairn who had slipped from his mount, while still riding his own horse to third place position during the afternoon's running of the first quiniela.

It was in the fourth that the Davis displayed his keen horsemanship. Coming into the home stretch some 100 yards from the finish, P. C. Pimothes "M..."

(See HERO on Page 8.)

— Guardian Picture
JUNIOR DAVIS
. . , Horseback Hero

March 23, 1954
Horseback Hero Saves Jockey from Trampling
Thirteen-Year-Old Lad Catches Rider When Saddle Slips

A hero on horseback was acclaimed Tuesday afternoon when Hobby Horse Hall's Personal Safety, the safety of leading jockey disregarded his mount and a purse for the owner of his mount to avert possible death to one of his fellow turf riders.

Junior Davis, a thirteen-year-old whose gallantry won the hearts of the many racing fans, sensationally held aloft Jockey Preston Nairn, who had slipped from his mount while still riding his own horse to third place position during the afternoon running of the first quiniela.

THE WEEKEND GUARDIAN SUNDAY

'Good News' Bursts Down Stretch To Win Race Track's Marathon Cup

April 10, 1954

Good News Burst Down Stretch to Win Racetrack Marathon Cup

Good News, cracking from the three-furlong post with a surprising burst of speed Friday afternoon, raced down Hobby Horse Hall's straight away to win the featured Marathon Cup Race before a record-breaking and astonished crowd.

It was the fourth triumph of the season for the three-year-old son of Fleet-foot, sired by George Melaxon, and it was his best as he turned in the longest run in good time of 2.56 9/10 minutes for the mile-and-a-half romp.

Owned by Bert A. Cambridge and trained by Harry Griffith, Good News was under Jockey G. Woodside for his trip and was a length ahead of D. McPhee's Gallant Miss, handled by Jockey A. "Moon" Ramsey. Third was W. A. Weeks's Boo Boo, ridden by leading jockey, J. "Droopy" Davis, some two lengths back.

There was a claim of foul against Good News, but it was disallowed by the race stewards, Mr. Patrick Broome, Mrs. Agnes Moore, Dr. Gordon Learn, and Dr. K. V. A. Rodgers.

Nassau's Leading Newspaper, Founded 1844—

CX. No. 117   THURSDAY   APRIL   22   1954   •   PRICE 3D.

Trainer Suspended, Owner Told to Refund Purse

Horse 'Drugged' In Marathon Race

The government-appointed Racing Commission revealed Wednesday a "stimulant" was used on "Good News"—the horse that charged to a 50-to-one victory in Hobby Horse Hall's marathon cup race two weeks ago. At the same time, the Commission revoked the licence of Trainer Harry Griffith and ordered Mr. B. A. Cambridge, former owner of "Good News", to return the £120 purse money and trophy he received after the race.

Thursday, April 22, 1954
Trainer Suspended; Owner Told to Refund Purse
Horse "Drugged" in Marathon Race

The government-appointed Racing Commission revealed Wednesday a stimulant was used on Good News––the horse that charged to a 50 to 1 victory in Hobby Horse Hall's Marathon Cup Race two weeks ago. At the same time, the commission revoked the license of trainer, Harry Griffith, and ordered Mr. Bert A. Cambridge, former owner of Good News, to return the £120 purse money and trophy he received after the race.

The Florida State Racing Commission chemical laboratory showed that the urine tests resulted in positive traces of nikethamide or a closely related compound. The 1954 riding champion, J. "Droopy" Davis, is the hero!

1954

His Excellency The Governor and countess of Ranfurly, shown at right were guests of Dr. Raymond W. Sawyer owner of the Race Course during one of the early meets of the current season. The Earl and Countess are shown with Dr. Sawyer helping themselves to the buffet lunch prepared by the Montague Beach Hotel.   Roland Rose Photo

Congratulations to Dr. Sawyer and the management of Hobby Horse Hall for the improved manner in which the track has been run this season.

1954 Season: Hobby Horse Hall Closed
after the Twenty-Sixth Meet
January 1955

Magic tourist figures for 1954: 109,605. That's how many tourists visited the colony for all-time new record. Track cleanup promised. Racing Commission chairman, George Baker, MHA, flatly told more than one hundred racehorse owners, trainers, grooms, and jockeys that the commission intends to stamp out foul practices at the track. Copies of the ninety-page rules of racing--newly revised regulations governing horse racing in the colony--were distributed.

Now that all of you have copies, ignorance of the rules will be no excuse.

January 8, 1955
Cole Resigns Post as Race Starter

Cole Resigns Post As Race Starter

Nassau's off-again, on-again racing controversy erupted Saturday with the disclosure that the Hon. A. K. Cole, who has been starting races in the Colony for more than 20 years, has resigned.

With the opening of the winter racing season due next Friday — only six days away — Hobby Horse Hall today is without an official starter.

At the same time came warnings of more trouble ahead. Rumours and reports, so far unofficial and unconfirmed, said that some horse owners would not enter their mounts in this year's race meet because of a disagreement with the Bahamas Racing Commission over the new rules and regulations.

The racing season will definitely open with a full programme on Friday, but the disagreement between the Racing Commission and some owners, jockeys and handlers is expected to continue for some time.

Mr. Cole, one of the best known figures in Nassau racing and horsemanship, revealed that he sent his resignation to the Racing Commission on Thursday because of the Commission's "uncompromising attitude."

He sent letters to that effect to Jerome Baker, M.H.A., Chairman of the Commission; Dr. R. W. Sawyer, M.H.A., President of the Montagu Park Racing Association, which owns Hobby Horse Hall; and L. C. Price, President of the Bahamas Race Horse Owners Association.

The Colony's Rules of Racing, as adopted by the
(See Cole Resigns, page 35)

A. K. Cole
resigns as starter

Nassau's off-again, on-again racing controversy erupted Saturday with the disclosure that Honorable A. K. Cole, who has been starting races in the colony for more than twenty years, has resigned. Mr. Cole sent his resignation letter to the commission on Thursday because of the commission's uncompromising attitude. Mr. William Turtle was appointed as the new race starter.

Twelve Are Eliminated from Race Roster as "Undesirables"

THE NASSAU GUARDIAN   Tuesday, Jan. 11, 1955

Horses of Hobby Horse Hall

SUNNY'S JEWEL — Very little can be said about Sunny's Jewel. But Newton Higgs' three-quarter bred three-year-old hopeful is among the better bred of young ponies at Hobby Horse Hall. The mare was nomi-nated once last season and ran out of the money. All reports say that the young racer has a very good time over the four furlong and will provide stiff competition for horses of her class. Jockey J. Stubbs is up.

—Guardian Photo by James Muir

The Bahamas Racing Commission, seeking to give horse racing in the colony a clean bill of health, rejected twelve applicants for licenses to participate in Nassau's 1955 racing season at Hobby Horse Hall, it was revealed Saturday.

£500 Reward

A reward of £500 will be paid to any person giving information to the management of Hobby Horse Hall that will lead to the prosecution and conviction of anyone tampering with the races in any way at Hobby Horse Hall.

Signed

Montagu Park Racing Association

The 1955 Racing Season Opens and Track Fans See Hope for Clean Racing

February 11, 1955
Three Horses Tumble in Fifth Race
Jockey Brice Suspended for Season

February 22, 1955
Movie Star Presents Cup

THE NASSAU GUARDIAN Wednesday, Feb. 23, 1955

MOVIE STAR PRESENTS' CUP—Ida Lupino presents the Fort Montagu Beach Hotel Cup to Jack Johnson who received the trophy for Newton Higgs, owner of winning horse "Sunny's Jewel." Her husband, actor Howard Duff is at left. The group, left to right; Mr. Duff, Mr. Johnson, Miss Lupino, jockey "Moon" Ramsey, and trainer Lawrence Lightbourn.
—Photo by William Wardel

First Tuesday'Meet

'Sunny's Jewel' Cops Montagu Cup

Bly Addington Cambridge

"Sunny's Jewel," three-year-old speed merchant of Skyline Stables, scored a romping triumph Tuesday in Hobby Horse Hall's featured six-furlong Fort Montagu Beach Hotel Champagne Cup Race before a small crowd at Nassau's mile-long racecourse.

Given a confident 'ride' by jockey A. "Moon" Ramsey, "Sunny's Jewel" won easily over Clifford Stalkart's "Dressel" and Felix Johnson's "Shirley."

"Sunny's Jewel" who earned the tall trophy also added another laurel to the fame of Ramsey—Hobby Horse Hall's leading jockey. In seven meets and 24 times up, Ramsey has a record of nine wins,

three seconds, three thirds, and nine also rans.

Toting 104 pounds, "Sunny's Jewel" was never challenged as he sprinted the six furlongs in the minute, 24 5/10 seconds. From the start of the race he led the nine-horse pack and was never pushed.

"Shirley" and "Dressel" put on an exciting 'show' for the fans when they battled it out in the home stretch. The struggle ended with "Dressel" proving the stronger and gaining second position in the classic run.

In the winner's circle in front of the Club House, film star Ida Lupino presented the trophy to Jack Johnson of Nassau Tours on behalf of Newton Higgs, owner of "Sunny's Jewel."

Trainer Lawrence Lightbourn, Ramsey and "Sunny's Jewel" also got into the picture as the group posed for photographers.

Immediately following ceremony champagne was served to the patrons of Hobby Horse Hall.

The day was also marked by long shot winners — Alfred Smith's "Tabu," 15-1; X. B. McGregor's "Theory," 15-1; Leonard Dames' "Tarzana," 10-1; A. Griffith's "Pampoon," 30-1 and Maria Lockhart's "Honey Love," 15-1.

The following are the parimutuel payoffs for the seven races:

First Race—Five Furlongs
Time: 1 min. 14.1 secs
1. Nola, 19s. 9d., 4d.
2. nous, 10s.—11s. 3d.
3. Sno Honey, 13s.

Second Race — Four Furlongs
Time: 56 secs.

Hobb Hall Daily Double
1. Tabu, 15s. 3d. 6s. 9d., 5s. 6d.
2. Stanlow, 23s. 9d.
3. All Star, 79s. 3d.

Third Race—Five Furlongs
Time: 1 min. 21 secs
Second Hall Daily Double
Theory, 15s. 9d., 9s. 3d., 5s. 3d.
Tarzana, 88s. 49s. 9d.
Eternal Dream, 21s. 3d.

Fourth Race — Five Furlongs
Time: 1 min. 21½ secs

First Quinella
Star Shoes, 35s. 3d., 29s. 5d
Caltex Malibu, 44s. 3d., 22s. 9d.
Lotus Indry, 52s. 3d.

Fifth Race — Six Furlongs
Time: 1 min. 24.1 secs
1. Second Quinella
1. Sunny's Jewel, 24s. 9d., 12s. 9d.
2. Dressel, 21s. 3d., 29s. 3d.
3. Shirley, 24s.

Sixth Race — Six Furlongs
Time: 1 min. 24 secs
1. Third Quinella
1. Recovery, 12s. 15s. 3d.
2. Jim Bunny, 37s. 3d.

Seventh Race — Six Furlongs
Time: 1 min. 24 secs
Fourth Quinella
1. Pampoon, 242s. 34s. 6d., 70s. 3d.
2. Geneine, 12s. 14s. 6d.
3. Honey Love, 39s. 3d.

Daily Double—Nos. 2 and 4, pays 377 10s. 6d.

First Quinella — Nos. 1 and 3, pay
120 29s. 3d.

Second Quinella—Nos. 1 and 4, pa
15 15s. 3d.

Third Quinella—Nos. 3 and 6, pa
11 4s. 3d.

Fourth Quinella—Nos 2 and 7, pa

Ida Lupino presented the Fort Montagu Beach Hotel Cup to Jack Johnson, who received the trophy for Mr. Newton Higgs, owner of winning horse, Sunny Jewel. Her husband, actor Howard Duff, also shared in the presentation. Sunny Jewel was ridden by Austin "Moon" Ramsey and trained by Lawrence "Fuzzy" Lightbourn.

April 1, 1955

For the first time in the history of the track, the daily double combination numbers were 9 and 9--Mrs. Irene Demeritte's Good News and A. Strachan's Sabre King. The racing fans always felt the combination was a jinx and would never play at Hobby Horse Hall.

Daily double 9 + 9 paid £13. 17s. 3d.

Joe Billy leads three-year-old field to capture Racing Commission Cup. The renowned son of Hobby Horse Hall's Hedron demonstrated his strength and stamina in the homestretch and finished the mile-long classic run in one minute, fifty-seven seconds ahead of A. F. Pindling's Temptation.

Mr. George Baker, MHA, chairman of the Racing Commission, presented the Commission's Cup to Mrs. Viola Greenidge, owner of Joe Billy. Mr. Baker said, without a good trainer and efficient jockey, there wouldn't be a winner. Joe Billy was brought to the Winner's Circle by trainer Arlington Shurland. In the saddle was Godfrey Woodside, Moon Ramsey rode Temptation to second place, and L. C. Brice's Shoo Fly, with Alfred Glinton, ran third.

April 5, 1955
Bill Leads Two-Year-Old by the Lengths

It took W. A. Weeks's Bill one minute and eleven seconds Tuesday to prove to Hobby Horse Hall fans that he is the track's champion two-year-old racer.

Horses of Hobby Horse Hall

"TEMPTATION" — The three-year-old hopeful of A. 'F'. Pindling's stables is among the better bred three-quarters of Hobby Horse Hall. Sired by the famed George Metaxon, a stallion imported from Jamaica and now at Exuma "Temptation" runs the four furlongs easily in 56 seconds. She first raced in the 1954 season when she had just turned two years but was never pushed by her handlers. She ran in four races of which she won one and was out the money three times. Much is expected of "Temptation" this season. She is being handled by trainer Lawrence Lightbourn. Jockey A. Ramsey is up and groom Carlton Lightbourn leads.

—Guardian Photo by James Muir

Overtaking a fast lead from A. F. Pindling's High Noon, the son of Hedron and Bonnie Lassie soon opened up a three-length lead over the field of eight.

With experienced jockey Alfred Glinton in the saddle, Bill was never challenged. High Noon, with the track's leading jockey, Austin "Moon" Ramsey, was second, and Chanel, third, ridden by J. Smith.

CUP RACE WINNER—Mrs. Claibourne Pe'l, left, presents the Mill River Stables Cup to Miss Carol Johnson, owner of "Princess Montagu," ridden by Austin Ramsey and trained by Hugh Strachan, right. (Guardian Photo by Addington)

Commission Cup Nomination

OUTSTANDING THREE-YEAR-OLD — L. C. Brice's three-quarter-bred "Shoo Fly" is one of Hobby Horse Hall's fastest sprinters. Nominated for the Racing Commission's Cup race for three-year-old horses at the track. "Shoo Fly" poses a threat and will be difficult to beat. Out of "Flicker" the fast-stepping "Shoo Fly" is sired by "Hedron," a stallion given to Hobby Horse Hall by J. F. C. Bryce, owner of the Mill River Stables, New York. Trained by William Armbrister, left, "Shoo Fly" has jockey Ralph Buchanan up.
—(Guardian Photo by Addington Cambridge)

Austin "Moon" Ramsey, Hobby Horse Hall champion jockey for 1955.

1956 Race Season
March 16, 1956

Hobby Horse Hall

Bill does it again. The spirited son of Hobby Horse Hall's Hedron won the three-year-old Racing Commission Cup Race. Owned by W. A. Weeks, trained by C. Morley, and ridden by H. Clarke.

April 6, 1956

It was a great pleasure Friday, April 6, to see two youngsters battle it out as they rode in the final seven-race program of Hobby Horse Hall.

They were Preston Nairn and Rudy Smith. Both jockeys rode for what they were worth, and the stakes were high: £100 purse and trophy.

Mrs. J. F. C. Bryce, sister of Huntington Hartford, owner of world-renowned Paradise Island, and her husband are horse lovers and owners of the famous Balcony House offered the £100 purse and cup as awards to the outstanding jockey. She was of the opinion that this added incentive would improve the riding at Hobby Horse Hall.

Approving Mrs. Bryce's suggestion, the Racing Commission set about keeping check on the jockeys' performance, conduct, and general deportment at the track.

Nairn won, but Smith is not to be overlooked.

In the final tally of past performances of jockeys, the results were as follows:

Between the two teenage riders

Nairn—twenty-seven wins, sixteen seconds, fifteen thirds, and fifty-seven also ran

Smith—twenty-four wins, twenty-two seconds, twenty-three thirds, and fifty-seven also ran

Nairn rode out of Lawrence and Carlton Lightbourn (father and son team) stables while Smith rode out of Harcourt Bastian and C. Moxey stables.

Mr. George Baker, chairman of the Racing Commission, said the commission was very grateful to Mr. and Mrs. J. F. C. Bryce's continued interest in the betterment of riding standards and racing at Hobby Horse Hall. He regretted that Mrs. Bryce was unable to be present for the ceremonies but was also happy to introduce Princess Radziwill, who would make the presentation to Jockey Nairn!

It is interesting to note that during a race in 1954 at Hobby Horse Hall, Jockey Nairn's saddle slipped and was saved by leading jockey, J. "Droopy" Davis, and now is the champion for the 1956 racing season (you can be what you want to be).

Mr. Sidney Brown was appointed racing starter for the 1957 racing season.

Hobby Horse Hall: Good Prospects for Bright Season

Ninety-Three Pounds (£93) Quiniela Caps HHH Opening Day

HHH Jockeys Compete for £100 Purse and Trophy

Morning Star and Gypsy, combination 4–5, under the guidance of diminutive jockey Zeke Rolle, Morning Star paid £24. 2s. 6d. for win, £23. 10s. 0d. to place and £1. 17s. 6d. to show.

Dr. Raymond Sawyer. President of Bahamas Race Co. LTD. Hosting a luncheon at Hobby Horse Hall Race Track. L.T.R. Dr. Sawyer, Mrs. Sawyer, Mr. Allen Roberts, Unidentified Gentleman, and Mrs. Adele Roberts.

They are off Friday, February 1, 1957, Shoo-Bill for the lead. Bill outstrides Beauty, settling an argument for fans. The race was the feature event of the day. It carried a great deal of sentiment!

First: Bill, ridden by I. Sands
Second: Beauty, ridden by W. Williams
Third: Shoo-Fly, ridden by E. Rolle

His Jewel won the one-mile feature race at Hobby Horse Hall, the Montagu Beach Hotel Cup. The cup was presented to Mrs. Viola Greenidge, owner of the horse, by Mr. John L. Coda, manager of the hotel. Zeke Rolle was the jockey and Joseph Rolle, the trainer.

Friday, February 22, 1957

HIS JEWEL won the one-mile feature race at Hobby Horse Hall yesterday afternoon for the Montagu Beach Hotel Cup. The cup was presented to Mrs. Leola Greenidge, owner of the horse, by Mr. John L. Cota, manager of the Montagu. Pictured above are Mrs. Greenidge, His Jewel with jockey 'Zeke' Rolle and trainer J. Rolle, and Mr. Cota.   —Tribune photo.

Mr. & Mrs. Walter Leland Cronkite Jr. CBS Evening News anchor for 19 years (1962-1981) enjoying a day at Hobby Horse Hall as the guest of Dr. Raymond Sawyer.

Alan Roberts and Mrs. Adele Roberts and friends enjoying a buffet lunch at Hobby Horse Hall.

JEEPERS CREEPERS poses for victory photo at Hobby Horse Hall yesterday with owner K. M. Thompson (with trophy), Jockey S. Brennen, trainer H. B u r r o w s and Mr. and Mrs Clarance Quinn of the Royal Victoria Hotel. *(Tribune Photo)*

Jeepers Creepers, owned by K. M. Thompson, captures Royal Victoria Hotel Trophy. S. Brennen was the jockey, and H. Burrows was the trainer.

Alfred "Uncle" Glinton was the champion for the 1957 race season.

Mr. Peter Graham Chairman Bahamas Racing Commission is seen presenting the Top Jockey of the Year Alfred "Auncle" Glinton with check and trophy for 1957 Race Season.

The 1958 racing season got off to a good start, but management problems, the general strike, and the racetrack burned down!

Sawyer Files Petition To Close Race Track

MR. FOSTER CLARKE, Attorney for Raymond W. Sawyer, publishes a notice in The Tribune today announcing the filing of a petition in the Supreme Court for winding up the affairs of the Montagu Park Racing Association. The petition will be heard by His Lordship the Chief Justice on February 11th at 10:30 a.m.

It was revealed on Thurs-day, January 23rd, that Alexis Nihon, Godfrey K. Kelly and Alice Nihon, Director of Montagu Park Racing Association, had addressed a letter to Peter Graham, Chairman of the Racing Commission, informing him that Dr. Raymond W. Sawyer had been removed as President of the Montagu Park Racing Association Ltd. from January 22nd.

It was revealed at the same

time that this year's license for racing at Montagu Park was granted by the Racing Commission on the condition that Dr. Sawyer remains President and Managing Director of the company.

It was also stipulated in the license that the doctor should retain such interest as he now has in the company and advise the Commission in case

(Continued on page 2)

RAYMOND SAWYER   ALEXIS NIHON

ENTRIES IN THE NEXT RACE are walked around paddock while spectators in the Jockey Club take a final look at their selections before crossing to the pari-mutuel windows to place their bets. Modern American Tote equipment is used and the pari-mutuel betting is under Government supervision. --Colyn Rees

Opening Day, January 10, 1958. Jockey Melvin Godet won five races and placed second once.

January 12, 1958

Nassau awoke on the morning of Sunday, January 12, to find itself in the first stages of the general strike in its history!

January 22, 1958

It was announced today that Alexis Nihon, Godfrey Kelly, and Alice Nihon, directors of Montagu Park Racing Association, have addressed a letter to Peter Graham, chairman of the Racing Commission, informing him that Dr. Raymond Sawyer has been removed as president of the Montagu Park Racing Association Ltd. from January 22, 1958, and Mr. Hubert Deal was appointed managing director of Hobby Horse Hall.

January 30, 1958

Dr. Raymond Sawyer files petition to close track.

Mr. Foster Clarke, attorney for Dr. Raymond W. Sawyer, publishes a notice in the *Tribune* announcing the filing of a petition to the Supreme Court for winding up the affairs of the Montagu Park Racing Association Ltd.

Appearing for Montagu Park Racing were the Honorable Eugene Dupuch, Messrs. Newton Higgs and Godfrey Kelly.

Mr. Leonard Knowles and Mr. Foster Clarke represented Mr. Sawyer.

February 1, General Strike Ends!

Monday, February 17, 1958

NIHON WINS TRACK CASE

An application by Dr. Raymond Sawyer to wind up the affairs of Montagu Park Racing Association was rejected this morning. The petition was thrown out by His Lordship the Chief Justice, Sir Guy McL. Henderson.

Appearing for Montagu Park were the Hon. E u g e n e Dupuch, Messrs. Newton Higgs and Godfrey Kelly.

Mr. Leonard Knowles and Mr. Foster Clarke represented Dr. Sawyer.

Following is the judgement of His Lordship the Chief Justice, Sir Guy McL. Henderson:

This is an application by way of petition under the Companies Act (Chapter 124 of the Laws of the Bahamas) to wind up the Montagu Park Racing Association Ltd. on the grounds that it is just and equitable that the Company should be wound up, thereby invoking the provisions of item (5) of section 79 of that Act. The petition was filed on the 28th January, 1958 by Dr. Raymond W. Sawyer, a shareholder in the Company. Notice of the filing was duly given on the 29th January and a date for hearing the petition was provisionally fixed for the 11th February. On the 6th February a supplementary affidavit was filed by Dr. Sawyer, a copy of which was apparently served upon Messrs. Higgs & Kelly, who, on the 8th February entered an appearance on behalf of Mr. Alexis Nihon, also a shareholder in the Company, opposing the petition. On the same day affidavits were filed by Mr. Nihon and also by Mr. Herbert A. Deal, a member of the firm of accountants Herbert A. Deal & Co. who have been the accountants for the Company from the year 1950 to date, and have had the business of compiling the balance sheets and annual accounts of the Company during that period. The matter could not be heard upon the advertised date but was eventually

(Continued on page six)

ALEXIS NIHON
President Montagu Park Racing Association

Horse Racing Feb. 28?

There may be horse racing at the scarred Hobby Horse Hall on Friday, February 28, if the Racing Commission lifts its ban.

A group of horse-owners met, with Mr. Herbert Deal, manager, and Mr. Alexis Nihon at the track this afternoon.

The possibility of flying tote machines in from Miami and the construction of a provisional building were discussed.

The horse-owners are working with the management towards this goal.

Nihon wins track case. The petition was thrown out by His Lordship, the chief justice, Sir Guy McL. Henderson.

FIRE FLATTENS TRACK

TWO FIRE BALLS BLAZE FOR HOURS

Estimated Loss £85,000

WHILE a Supreme Court battle raged between the shareholders of the Montagu Park Racing Association, Nassau's 25-year-old race course caught fire last night — and burned to the ground.

The estimated damaged at Montagu Park Racing Association is £85,000. This morning Mr. Alison Nihon, President of Montagu Park, and legal adviser Mr. Newton Higgs went to the Criminal Investigation Department and made a formal request for an extensive investigation on the cause of fire.

Within an hour, the two balls of fire which shot up

Fire flattens track. Two fireballs blaze for hours. Estimated loss is £85,000.

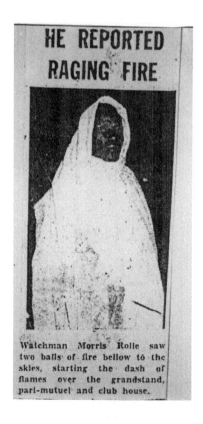

HE REPORTED RAGING FIRE

Watchman Morris Rolle saw two balls of fire bellow to the skies, starting the dash of flames over the grandstand, pari-mutuel and club house.

Watchman Morris Rolle reported raging fire on Sunday night, February 16. Building of Hobby Horse Hall, Nassau's only racetrack was reduced to a skeleton by flames last night. None of the racehorses were injured.

February 28, 1958

Now

£2,000

Immediately after the fire at Hobby Horse Hall Sunday night Mr. Alexis Nihon, President of Montagu Park Racing Association, offered a reward of £1,000 for information leading to the arrest and conviction of any person who may have started the fire.

Today he doubles the reward —he has upped it to £2,000.

A group of horse owners met with Mr. Herbert Deal, manager, and Mr. Nihon at the track to discuss the possibility of flying tote machines in from Miami and the construction of a provisional building. Management decided not to resume racing to the dismay of the horse owners!

The 1958 racing season came to a sad ending. Melvin Godet was the leading jockey with five wins and one second after one race meet.

November 1958

The House of Assembly voted not to renew the license of Alexis Nihon and Montagu Park Racing Association Ltd.

Dr. Raymond Sawyer abstained from voting.

1959

The Nassau Beach Hotel opens, owned and operated by the Crothers brothers.

The Bahamas government granted Bahamas Raceco Ltd. a racing license to operate Hobby Horse Hall Racetrack. Dr. R. W. Sawyer, president and managing director; Mr. Richard Wright of Coral Gables, director.

Construction work had started on the Turf Club.

The £75,000 investment for renovation and modernization covered the installation of new tote machines, photo finish cameras, vehicles, and ten gate electric starting gates of American design. The one-mile racecourse itself was given a spruce up to provide better and safer running conditions. The track was weeded, topped, graded, dragged, and rolled.

Bahamians should boycott the opening of the racetrack, front-page story of the *Herald*. Mr. Cyril Stevenson, editor and close friend of Alexis Nihon, felt that Mr. Nihon was not treated fairly as his license to operate Hobby Horse Hall was not renewed.

Early in the fifties, Mr. Nihon offered Mr. Cyril Stevenson, editor of the *Herald*, £1,000 if he didn't touch a drink of alcohol for one year!

1960

Horse racing return is great success.

Horse Racing's Return Is Great Success

BY MORGAN GOODWIN

HOBBY HORSE HALL, flashing its new smile, ushered in the 1960 racing season on January 8th with a smashing success. An estimated 3,000 persons attended the track opening which marked the end of a two-year lapse in Nassau Parimutuel Racing.

His Excellency the Governor, Sir Raynor Arthur, K.C.M.G., C.V.O., and Lady Arthur topped a huge list of local dignitaries, officials and other prominent guests on hand for the first day of wagering.

Greeting the guests at the newly re-built Cable Beach Sporting Palace which replaces the former one gutted by fire were spacious Club House accommodations, grand stand, attractive white fencing and numerous other eye-catching facilities.

Construction work has been accomplished with an eye for retaining charm, atmosphere and excitement of previous meetings with a new setting of maximum comfort and convenience to race goers, according to the Hon. Dr. Raymond W. Sawyer, Nassau dentist and member of the Bahamas House of Assembly who is Managing Director of Bahamas Racoco, Ltd.

The £75,000 investment for renova-

tion and modernization covered the installation of New Tote Machine, Photo Finish Cameras, Vehicles and a Ten-Gate Electric Starting Gate of American design. The one-mile race course itself was also given a spruce-up to provide better and safer running conditions. The track was weeded, topped, graded, dragged and rolled.

Opening day guests enjoyed cocktails and a buffet catered by the Montagu Beach Hotel which will continue this service on the ground patio throughout the season which ends April 19. Bahamian youngsters, who make up the jockey corps, will ride on Tuesdays and Fridays for followers of "The Sport of Kings".

(More photographs on pages 26, 27)

ARRIVING AT HOBBY HORSE HALL for the opening day of racing were, left to right, Sir Raynor Arthur, Governor of the Bahamas, the Hon. Dr. Raymond W. Sawyer, M.E.C., M.H.A., president of Bahamas Rogaco, Ltd., and Lady Arthur.

—Roy Newbold, Jr.

Hobby Horse Hall, flashing its new smile, ushered in the 1960 racing season on January 8 with smashing success. An estimated three thousand persons attended the track opening, which marked the end of a two-year lapse in Nassau's pari-mutuel betting.

His Excellency the Governor, Sir Raynor Arthur, KCMG, CVO, and Lady Arthur topped a huge list of local dignitaries, officials, and other prominent guests on hand for the first day of racing. Ms. Caroline Arthur, daughter of the governor and Lady Arthur, and chief justice of the Bahamas, Sir Guy Henderson, KT, QC, Mr. Richard Wright, Racing Commission chairman, Mr. Peter Graham, MHA, and Mr. John Oldfield of Coral Gables, Florida, were in attendance.

Return of Horse Racing

—Roy Newbold, Jr.

MRS. JOHN BARON, centre, at Hobby Horse Hall with her house guests,
Mr. and Mrs. Neil Carnsew, newly-weds from Montreal. Below, picking a
winner were, left to right, Mrs. John F. McCarthy, Mrs. Gordon W. Aitken
and her daughter Patricia, of Glen Rock, N. J. and Nassau.

—Roy Newbold, Jr.

MRS. HARLEY EARL, Palm Beach, whose husband is the former vice-president
of General Motors, chats with Mr. Henry S. Woodard, Delray Beach, Fla.,
and Mrs. Bradner Lee, of Los Angeles.

182

Nassau Polo Association Banquet
20th April 1960

Seated at the head of the table:

1. Sir Guy W. Mc L. Henderson
Chief Justice of the Bahamas

Seated on the left side from
the front go back are:

Seated on the right side from
the back go front are:

1. N. James French
2. Harcourt Maura
3. L. Lightbourne
4. A. G. Roberts
5. A. K. Cole

1. A. M. Moore
2. A. B. Malcolm
3. G. Garfukel
4. S. C. Pyfrom
5. A. J. Dew
6. C. G. Damianos

Pictured above are left to right: Dr. Unger, representative of the American College of Allergists, who presented the Bahamas Conference Trophy to MR. Arindale Griffith owner of Mischief, Jockey Joseph Smith and trainer Harry Griffith.

(Tribune Photo)

Arlington Miller (left) owner of Modest Maiden, receives handsome trophy from Mr. Scothy Anderson, manager of British Colonial, yesterday at Hobby Horse Hall, when his horse finished first over such favourites as Steplight, Red Label and Mark Twain. In the irons is Jockey Joseph Smith while trainer Glenroy Evans look on.

(Tribune Photo)

1961

Ladies Day at Hobby Horse Hall

L.R. Angela Archer – Dr. Raymond Sawyer – Miss Deschmps and Joan Dupuch Munning.

Mrs. Lori Whitehead rode Bahamian Gal to a photo finish victory in the Ladies Race. Sir Roland Symonette presented the trophy. The Ladies Race was the highlight of the day's program. Dignitaries attending the races were Mr. Justice Campbell and his daughters, Victoria, Mrs. Kay St. George, the Honorable John Barnard, United States consul general in the Bahamas, and Mrs. Barnard, Lady Symonette, and Mrs. Harold Johnson were in attendance.

--Roy Newbold, Jr.

MRS. LORI WHITEHEAD, above, winner of the Ladies' Race prepares to accept her prize from Sir Roland Symonette. Mrs. Whitehead rode to a photo-finish victory on Bahamian Gal, owned by K. G. Richie.

Sir Roland with Dr. Raymond Sawyer, right, managing director of the company which operates the track, and Miss Vivian Vance and Mr. John Baragrey of the Playhouse.

The Hon. John L. Barnard and Mrs. Barnard before the start of the Ladies' Race. Mr. Barnard is the United States Consul General in the Bahamas.

Mr. Justice Campbell escorts his daughter, Victoria, left and Mrs. Kay St. George to the paddock to pick a winner in the Ladies Race at Hobby Horse Hall.

LADY SYMONETTE, left, discusses the races at Hobby Horse Hall with the wife of the Governor of the Bahamas, Lady Stapledon. Ladies' Race was the highlight of the day's programme.

–Roy Newbold, Jr.

Dr. Sawyer, managing director of Raceco Ltd has an attentive audience in His Excellency the Governor, second from left, and Raceco shareholders Mr. William Wright and Mr. Noland Johnson, both of Florida.

Lady Stapledon, right, enjoying the afternoon of racing with Mrs.
Harold Johnson, centre, and Mrs. Raymond Sawyer.

—Roy Newbold, Jr.

CHARLIE (DIAMOND KID) GIBSON

Today's Personality has just made history in horse racing circles in England. He is an "All Bahamian" boy, 18 years of age and known as "The Diamond Kid".

Charlie Gibson is "The Diamond Kid" and he received this name as a result of his services to the K. M. Thompson stables which colours are black shirt with a gold diamond. He was sent to England in early May to receive further jockey training from top jockeys and trainers. After only six weeks of training there he got his coveted jockey's license from the exclusive Jockey Club.

Charlie becomes the first Negro ever to ever receive his jockey's license from the Jockey Club in England. News of this Commission's success reached Nassau this week from Mr. Reginald Johnson, owner of several of England's top race horses.

Mr. Johnson went on to say "The Diamond Kid" is riding much better than he ever rode in Nassau. He should really be like shown in front of those stable boys on the island of New Providence next season", He also stated that Charlie is very well liked by all who meet him. In fact he stated that Mr. Thompson has taken the Bahamian youth into his own home to live with his family.

Mr. Hannon is the owner and operator of the well known "Hannon Stables" in Everleigh, Hampshire, England. It is at these stables that Charlie is receiving his training.

Young Gibson had a good record here at the end of the last horse racing season at Hobby Horse Hall. He recorded 28 wins; 27 seconds; and 12 third positions. This turned out to be one of the best scores at Hobby Horse Hall last season.

CHARLIE GIBSON

He made history when he went to England. He was the first Bahamian rider ever to travel there to receive further training in this field. Now Mr. Johnson writes his friends here in Nassau to report that Charlie is successful in his training, in making friends among the English people, and in giving them good impressions of the way Bahamians live.

"The Diamond Kid" has only been riding for two years. He was discovered by his uncle Henry Burrows, who trained him and took him to live with him at his residence in Coconut Grove. His uncle now proudly says: "I always felt Charlie could be a great rider some day. I can hardly wait until next season to see the improvements he has made."

Mr. Johnson jokingly says "Charlie will be able to teach his Uncle Henry a thing or two about training and riding when he returns to Nassau."

Charlie Gibson is expected to return here about the end of November. Immediately he will begin training for the forthcoming season at Hobby Horse Hall. Between now and November the Bahamian will pit his skill against that of well trained English riders.

Charlie "Diamond" Gibson

Is seen with his tack at "Hannon Stables" in Everleigh, Hampshire, England. It is at these stables that Charlie got his training.

Day at the Races 1961, Easter Monday. L. to R. Arnold Flowers Jr., Ivan "Abaco" James, Willie Minnis, and Basil "Six" Francis.

Lady Sassoon is seen presenting the Lord Carnavon Cup to Mr. Victor Claridge owner of the winning horse "ZORICH" trained by Mr. Walker is seen holding "ZORICH" Bridle.

It is interesting to note that in England's Racing History, Sir Victor Sassoon as owner and breeder of race horses won England's most prestigious horse race the Epsom Derby four times in eight years. 1953 "Pinza" ridden by Sir Gordon Richards and Norman Brite was the trainer. This was Sir Gordon Richards's first Epson Derby win in twenty eight mounts. 1957 "Crepello" ridden by Lester Piggot, trainer Noel Murless. In 1958 "Hard Ridden" ridden by C. Smirke and Mick Rogers was the trainer and in 1960 "St. Paddy" ridden by L. Piggott with Noel Murless as the trainer. Sir Victor Sassoon love and passion to breed and race horses, it was noted after his death he requested that Lady Sassoon continue to race and breed horses not to spend her time controlling the Sassoon banking business.

1961

Angela Archer whips "Cochise" to second place in the ladies race.

1962

Jockey QuBell Rolle Hand Ride "Galedo II" owned by Mr. Sidney French to the finish line all alone.

Dr. Raymond Sawyer right President of Bahamas Raceo, Ltd., escorts
Sir Robert Stapledon, Governor of the Bahamas and Lady Stapledon as
they arrive to attend the races at Hobby Horse Hall 1962 Racing Season.
William Roberts Photo

Trainer Melvin Godet walks Joan Dupuch
Munnings to the starting gate.

In the winning circle – Mrs. Joan Dupuch Munnings atop Ashton Demeritte's "Rattler" displays the trophy presented to her by Sir Roland Symonette, the Bahamas first Premier, as trainer Melvin Godet looks on, the presentation was made for her championship ride in the ladies Amateur Cup Race at Hobby Horse Hall on Friday.

Dr. Raymond Sawyer looks on as Mr. Charlie Major Senior Racing Commission Member presents: Alfred "Uncle" Glinton with the Wining Jockey of the Year Award.

Raceco's president, Dr. Raymond Sawyer, states the total costs of the new improvements accomplished since last season exceeded £10,000 ($28,000), and he also stated that of the $3.15 clubhouse admission and $1.40 grandstand admission, the Bahamas government will receive 10 percent in addition to 7 percent of the total handle.

Monies derived under this system by the government in the past two years have built seven (7) new Out Island medical clinics and provided considerable medical services to the Bahamian people (now that is very, very interesting).

1962–1963

Charlie "The Diamond Kid" Gibson a top his mount, the Hot Walker is Henry Burrows and in the back ground a top his mount Mr. B the No Nonsense R. Peterson.

Colin Rees

Ronald Strachan's Bold Weevil, Mike Darville's Miss Omolene, and K. M. Thompson's Asavache were the then outstanding Bahamian-bred racehorses. Miss Omolene, she was the queen of racing.

1964

Tuesday, April 14, Borasco scores easy win in Horse of the Year Cup Race.

THE NASSAU DAILY TRIBUNE

Cindy Wins Confidential Club Cup Race

Jockey Q. Martin sits proudly in Cindy's saddle as Meredith Thompson holds the trophy his brother's horse won in the feature race at Hobby Horse Hall yesterday. Mr. Nelson Chipman, operator of the Confidential Club, who donated the trophy is at left. Trainer George Christie is on the right.

The "Asavache" Cup

Senator K. M. Thompson is seen presenting the Asavache cup to Mr. Victor Claridge owner of the winning horse "Zorich".

Tribute To My Dad Senator K.M. Thompson (deceased)

As far back as I can remember, my father K. M. Thompson Sr. always loved animals and passed that love on to us. There had always been animals in our lives but horses were my father's favorite. He arose early each morning to see that the horses were groomed and fed properly before he opened his business I-Need-A Laundry. The stables were at the rear of the business so he could check in on them during the day.

We would ride as a family each Sunday, all dressed in our riding habits. This ceased when mother was expecting my sister Marlene. I still rode each morning before school, to the Monastery and back. After school each afternoon I would ride again. We each owned our own horse. My horse was Don Lopez, Merediths (my brother) was Conya Barvo and Marlene's was Dashra. When they were not training for racing we had to care for them ourselves grooming, feeding and exercising.

When our mares were due to foal my father would lean against the stable wall and keep on asking the vet if there wasn't anything he could do to relieve the mares' discomfort. didn't want to see them suffer.

In order to improve the blood lines in the Bahamas, Daddy imported thorobreds from Ocala and Kentucky. There was Homely Duke, son of Gallant Duke who had raced in the 1942 Kentucky Derby. He was ridden by Eddie Arccaro. They didn't win but was a participant. Homely Duke has a son Little Paul who won a 2 mile race at Rioduso Downs in New Mexico.

Gay Bain who still rides in Florida was our main jockey. He rode Asavache, Borrasco etc. Other jockeys were Austin Saunders, Q-Martin, K. Glinton Godet, A Glinton to name a few. Our trainers were Naddy, Geo, Christie, J. Marshall, Develand Deveaux, Geo Greenslade and Henry Burrows (not all at the same time).

Daddy enjoyed winning – not necessarily monetary wise, but to know he had bred a foal fed it well, trained it and have it become a great winner like Asavache was all the reward he wanted. He was proud of his horses win or lose.

Later on in his racing careers my father bought 2 beach front lots and 20 acres to the rear, where he built stables to house his ever growing number of horses. There they swam, and exercised on the long stretch of beach. They lived there in the summer only when they returned to town and the race track.

It was a part of my heritage I'll treasure always. It was so unpredictable, a time of suspense, excitement and enjoyment. When you spent an afternoon having lunch, making a few small wages and socializing with friends, you felt good when it was over. Especially of your horse won! One that you owned!

Kay Thompson

204

Meredith Thompson's Borasco barrelled into the home turn with more reserve than a three-stage rocket to run down Mike Darville's Miss Omolene and score an easy triumph in the Horse of the Year Cup Race. To the tumultuous roars of "Let Borasco catch that" from the clubhouse, Miss Omolene carried the race for about six and a half furlongs with Borasco some four lengths behind Bold Weevil. Zorich and Joe Grammatico's Coast Guard of the five horses field were some ten lengths of the pace.

As the powerful dark-gray stallion took the home turn, still four lengths behind Miss Omolene, B. Paul shifted Borasco into high gear, pulled beside the tall brown mare, and took the lead. Charlie "Diamond Kid" Gibson, mounted on Miss Omolene, staged a strong comeback bid after being overtaken by smart maneuvering by Paul punched a hole in Gibson's hope. Miss Omolene ran second and Ronald Strachan's three-year-old champion, Bold Weevil, third. Borasco was trained by C. "Slim" Deveaux.

Northern Dancer winner of The Kentucky Derby 1964

E.P. Taylor with Northern Dancer and Trainer Horatio Luro.
(Photo Courtesy Terry Conway)

The 1964 racing season ends.

Winner Of Horse Of The Year Cup Race

At the final meet of the 1964 horse racing season yesterday, top jockey Charley (Diamond Kid) Gibson, holding his trophy and a cheque for £100, is flanked by Dr. K.-V. A. Rodgers, left, of the Racing Commission and the Commission's Chairman.

Mr. Basil McKinney, who made the presentations to Gibson and D. (Hardcat) Martin. Martin at right was awarded £25 for his clean and co-operative racing records. See page 14 for full story.   (Tribune Photo)

15/4/64

THE VERY GOOD OLD DAYS AT
HOBBY HORSE HALL RACE TRCK
YOU NEVER KNOW WHAT YOU
GOT UNTIL YOU LOSE IT

IN THE WINNER'S CIRCLE - Miss Omoline retained her championship status in the Asavache Memorial Cup Race which was originated last year by Mr. K. M. Thompson, owner of one of the best locally bred horses ever to race at HHH and which died last year. On Friday, Miss Omoline set the pace from start to finish over nine furlongs with Jockey B. Paul enjoying a comfortable ride.

Left to right are Mr Meredith Thompson, who made the presentation of the trophy on behalf of his sick father; Mrs. Thompson; Mr. Mike Darville, Owner of Miss Omoline, with his trophy; Paul and Miss Omoline, and trainer Melvin Godet. (Photo by King Ingraham)

DALE STAR

TERMITE

RAMBLING ROSE

Charlie "Diamond Kid" Gibson, champion jockey, received a check for £100 and a trophy. D. "Hardcat" Martin was awarded £25 for his clean and cooperative racing records.

THE NASSAU DAILY TRIBUNE, NASSAU, N.P., BAHAMAS, SATURDAY, FEBRUARY 20, 1965

Racing Commission, Mr. Brian Snow, Racing Secretary, Mr. Harcourt Bastian, Handicapper and Dr. R. W. Sawyer, operator of Hobby Horse Hall.
—Tribune Photo.

AT RIGHT:—Magistrate S. Tupper Bigelow, Q.C., chairman of the Ontario Racing Commission, is shown second from left yesterday watching the races at Hobby Horse Hall with friends and members of the government supervised Bahamas Raceco Ltd. Sitting in front row are Mr. and Mrs. John Hooper of Toronto. In the centre row from left are Mrs. Gordon Boughner, Mr. Bigelow, Mr. K. G. Malcolm and Dr. K. V. A. Rodgers, both of the Bahamas Racing Commission. Standing from left are Mr. Charles Major of the

Mike Darville's light-bay mare, Miss Omolene, will be greatly missed for the 1965 race season. She fell in late April right after the close of the 1964 season, broke her back, and had to be shot!

During the months of September and October after the racing season, the trainers start to prepare horses for the upcoming race season.

Photo by Frederic Maura
Even race horses enjoy a swim.

The horses are catched up, wormed, and they go in training to sustain their fitness throughout the race season. Horse stables are repaired, with new bedding for the horses, and from October to April, Fuzzy Lightbourn's kitchen was the meeting place for a good stew fish and racetrack gossip for clockery, grooms, trainers, and jockeys and stable boys alike.

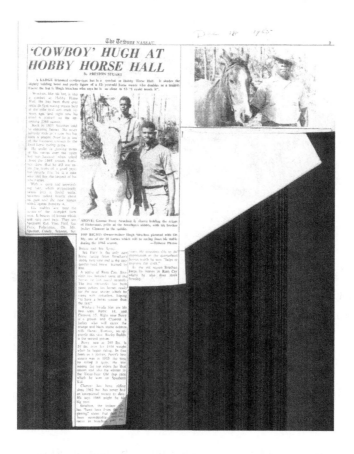

Legendary trainer Hugh "Cowboy" Strachan was an exercise boy during the Murphy's track days in the '30s. He never actually rode in a race but was noted to be a good groom.

THE NASSAU DAILY TRIBUNE, NASSAU,

COAST GUARD WINS THE ASAVACHE

Charley Gibson, riding a well-judged race, shot to the lead in the last furlong to win the Asavache Memorial Cup on "Coast Guard" at Hobby Horse Hall yesterday in a time of one minute, 53 seconds.

The horse is owned by Joe Gramatico, who was not pres-ent to receive the handsome trophy from Mr. Meredith Thompson, son of the Hon. Senator K. M. Thompson, who donated the trophy.

Shown at left from left to right are Mr. Meredith Thomp-son, Mrs. K. M. Thompson, Mrs. Meredith Louis Gramatico, w the trophy on be brother, Charlie "Coast Guard"

Mr. Aaron Knowle

—(Trib

He became one of the foremost trainers in the local horse racing game. His stable consisted of ten (10) horses--Fisherman, Oh My, Seaman, Tom Fool, Sea Fury, Spankers, Spaghetti Kidd, and Candy. His son Clement is the jockey for the stable, and his brother Perry, the groom for the stable.

Louis Grammatico's Coast Guard won the A. Savache Memorial Cup Race.

Groom Johnny Adderley was seen with the imported quarter bred. He is what everyone going to the races will want--tons of money.

Preston Stuart looks ahead to January 4, 1966.

Hobby Horse Hall has a £25,000 face-lift for the new season.

The Tribune NASSAU.   Dec 11 1965   13

Preston Stuart looks ahead to January 4

Hobby Horse Hall has a £25,000 facelift for new season

THERE final weeks before the January 4 opening date of the new 1966 horse racing season at Hobby Horse Hall are being spent to complete a £25,000 renovation which will present a new look at the Cable Beach race course while presenting several innovations.

Though the same course, building, and racing principles will be used and several practices are expected to remain standard, patrons will observe a new look as a result of the proposed changes.

Outsiders will not be able to watch the wagering of punters on the inside. A tall concrete wall around the entire paddock area will take care of this.

Bettors will not be able to leave the Clubhouse grounds to follow horses and jockeys as they leave the paddock for the starting gate. A new enclosed tote-gate has been installed and anyone leaving the gate will have to pay a second entrance fee.

CAMERA

The camera patrol system which was introduced at the end of this season, will be in full operation to image patrons of close races or otherwise jostle to convict jockeys who do not ride fair. Eight minutes after the race, Stewards will be shown a film of the entire race.

All this is being done because as Dr. Raymond Sawyer, operator of the government-supervised racing programme puts it "we have respect for the public and make arrangements for them".

Last opening date, January 3 of this year, a record crowd of 1,503 racing fans turned out and net opening date receipts of over £17,000.

Dr. Sawyer is looking forward to another record opening day. He says "when we open this year we will have the finest race plan in the world".

The 20-meet season will run until April 18.

Next Friday a session of track races will be held in the afternoon which is being held primarily to familiarise the staff. Dr. Sawyer said 6 or 8 horses will actually start and race. The public is invited to watch these races.

MAJOR CHANGE

There has been a major change affecting the patrons. Charles Lowe Jr. has been appointed handicapper in place of Harcourt "Gordy" Bartlett who will be training next year. Ordi Smith will take over Mr. Lowe's old job as clerk of the scales.

There will be four government Stewards who are Mr. Irvin Wechsler, Mr. Maurice Kelly, Mr. Marvel Waugh and Mr. C. G. Richardson.

Deputy Stewards are Mr. Etienne Dupuch Jr., Mr. Charles Lennox, Mr. Fox Leon and Mr. Eric Fisher.

Mr. Adrian Christoffle, Mr. Basil Ingraham, Mr. Vivian Mair and Mr. George Seeley are deputy Stewards. Mr. Sydney French is racing secretary and Mr. Garth Kemp, paramutuel manager.

Paddock Judge is Mr. Abbie Lloyd while Mr. Sam Patton is jockey room master. Starter is Mr. Albert Lloyd Jr.

The camera patrol system will be managed by Toogood) and Mr. King Ingraham remains as photo-finish expert.

The Big Bamboo again has the concession for the restaurant and bar services for the Clubhouse while Mr. Leo Phillips has been granted a similar concession for the Grandstand.

SECURITY

The private detective firm of Trace Limited will provide day and night security for the season.

The Racing Commission is chairmaned by Mr. Basil McKinney and include Mr. Charles Major, Mr. Howard Johnson, Dr. K. V. A. Rodgers and Mr. K. G. Malcolm.

The track has already been property graded and new padd

dock barns installed. For the 1966 season a total of 60 imported quarter bred horses were brought in.

Mr. French reports that only about 20 has arrived for the up-coming season and that the number of trainees left off from 20 down to 18. He added that there will be about 10 new local bred horses making their debut in 1966.

For the further protection of grantees the commission hires samples from all winning horses and from those who did not perform as expected, to send abroad for analysis.

The management still reserves the right to refuse admission to Hobby Horse Hall without assigning any reason for doing so and remove anyone from the premises under similar conditions.

DR. RAYMOND W. SAWYER
. . . operator

SYDNEY FRENCH
. . . racing secretary

TURNOUT FOR MOCK RACE POINTS TO A
RECORD SEASON IN 1966

BY PRESTON STUART

The enthusiasm generated at a mock race held at Hobby Horse Hall on Sunday points toward another record breaking attendance for the up coming 1966 season.

Hundreds of patrons, took a time out from their regular weekend activities to view the race which was held to familiarize the staff with the new tote system.

Although there was no wagering the Club house was almost packed to capacity and several people were even seen wearing binoculars.

There was a disappointment of many of these loyal patrons. Only one race was held and it was contested over one furlong.

Charley Gibson, top jockey in 1964 and 1965, got the fast starting gate in fine style and easily piloted him to a slim victory over Lady Smith on the short sprint.

The speed of posting returns, times and payoffs was almost unbelievable. Within three minutes they appeared on the tote board.

The new board, one of the major new additions incorporated in a £25,000 facelift at Hobby Horse Hall, was installed by Mr. Bill Patch of Baltimore, Maryland, of American Totalisator, and will be maintained by Mr. M. A. Ursillo of Miami, electrical engineer of American Totalisator, and will fly into Nassau on race days, explained the operations at Hobby Horse Hall.

Mr. Ursillo, who is based in Miami but will fly into Nassau on race days, explained the operations of the new system yesterday.

He said similar installations in the United States has handled billions of dollars of wagering and is guaranteed for its accuracy.

Mr. Ursillo said that basically, "It is an electrical system where money is recorded during the betting period in the

tote room."

He explained that after a seller punches a combination and before the ticket is issued, it is recorded by the system which consists of counters for each of the possible combinations in each race.

Mr. Ursillo said the system also records the number and total of bets made in each race. The odds for each horse is computed by the amount of bets placed on each entrant.

He said there are two small counting machines which

are being used for win, place and show betting and for quinella betting.

Mr. Garth Kemp, parimutuel manager, had a hectic day settling his staff but appears prepared to handle wagers.

M. A. URSILLO

The new tote board which has been installed by American Totalisator and will flash results minutes after race is completed.
—Tribune P

These final weeks before the January 4 opening date of the new 1966 horse racing season at Hobby Horse Hall are being spent to complete a £25,000 renovation, which will project a new look at the Cable Beach Racecourse.

Major Change: Sidney French, Racing Secretary

Charles Lunn Jr. has been appointed handicapper in place of Cordy Bastian, who will be training horses for the 1966 race season.

SERENADING — At Hobby Horse Hall Race Track, the smooth sounds of a Calypso band put fans in the proper frame of mind to bet. Their happy tunes also make losing that much easier.

Garth Kemp, pari-mutuel manager

GATE KEEPERS AND RACE FANS

There will be four (4) government stewards: Mr. Irwin Wechsler, Mr. Maurice Kelly, Mr. Marcel Waugh, and Mr. C. C. Richardson.

WATCHING FOR TIPS — Racing fans lined the fences on Saturday as the horses and jockeys paraded out, hoping to catch a winning tip. This is a familiar scene prior to every race as the horses head for the track.

The deputy stewards were as follows: Mr. Etienne Dupuch Jr., Mr. Charles Lehman, Mr. Tex Lunn, and Mr. Eric Fisher.

Members of the Racing Commission were as follows: Mr. Basil McKinney, chairman, Mr. K. G. Malcolm, Dr. K. V. A. Rodgers, Mr. Charles Major, and Mr. Howard Johnson.

Starter: Mr. Albert Lloyd

CHECKING THE HORSES — Popular local figures, from left, Felix "Mailman" Bowe, William "Life" Curtis and Donald "Nine" Rolle think over the horses before placing bets at the race track on Saturday.

Mr. Basil McKinney chairman of the Racing Commission of the Bahamas congratulates Jockey Alfred Auncie Glinton as the Second Leading Jockey for 1966 Race Season. Mr. Nelson Chipman looks on cheerfully!

Outsider Yama Wins Trophy Race
Waiting Game Pays Off for Jockey Eneas

Railbirds are shown watching the finish as jockey Cleveland Eneas and YAMA hit the tape in one minute and 55-seconds to score a four length victory

1966

Mr. Basil McKinney Chairman of Bahamas Racing Commission right is presenting Mrs. Ethlea Strachan owner of "Yama" the winning horse. Mr. Junior Lunn center racing Handicapper and Mr. Charles Major member Bahamas Racing Commission looks on.

Mr. David "Doc" Strachan Trainer of the Winning Horse "Yama"

Jockey Cleveland Eneas took a backseat view of the commemorative Trophy Race at Hobby Horse Hall for the first six (6) furlongs, watching the sprinters burn themselves out, then gunned Ethlea Strachan's Yama to a four-length win in the mile-feature fifth race event, which honored the two-day visit of Her Royal Highness Queen Elizabeth and her husband, Prince Philip.

Quiniela combination: 5–8, Yama–Volterra, which refunded a staggering £95. 5s. 3d. Miss Potter ran third.

Mr. Basil Mckinney Presents Charlie Gibson with his trophy as top jockey of 1966 Race Sason.

'Diamond Kid' To Ride On Cincinnati Track

By GUARDIAN REPORTER

CHARLEY GIBSON, the Racing Commission's top jockey for the 1966 Season left yesterday by Bahamas Airways for Cincinnati to ride at River Downs track there.

Charley is expected to start riding next week. He will be riding for Mr. Oscar Dishman, a horse owner and trainer. Mr. Dishman lives in Lexington, Kentucky, but he is now training in Cincinnati.

River Downs is a one-mile track with turf course and is at 6301 Kellogg Avenue, Cincinnati. It is completely modernized from 1955. The racing season starts late May and continues to early September. The track at River Downs seats 8,500 in the grandstand and 2,500 in the clubhouse section.

POTENTIAL

Dr. Archie Donaldson, a Bahamian who has been living in the United States for a number of years made the arrangements for young Gibson to ride abroad. Before Dr. Donaldson went off to school to study for his medical degree he expressed the belief that there was great potential for local jockeys in international competition. While watching the jockeys

CHARLEY GIBSON

ride in the States he was even more convinced that our local jockeys could measure up to foreign standards.

As a result, he contacted his brother, George D. Donaldson in Nassau and told him of the idea and asked if he could find a jockey who was deserving of a trial. Charley was the natural choice.

Dr. Donaldson came to Nassau about three months ago along with his wife, Dr. Shirley Donaldson, and after talking with Gibson he was quite pleased and made all the necessary arrangements.

DIAMOND

Charley is better known as "Diamond Kid" — a name which originated while riding for the K. M. Thompson stables whose colours were red with black diamond or black with red diamond.

Charley posted quite an impressive record for the 1966 season; he had 48 wins, 37 seconds, 26 thirds and 63 also ran. He has been the top jockey of Hobby Horse Hall for the past three seasons. In 1966 he broke Ezekiel Rolle's record for most wins for a season. Rolle's record was 42 wins.

Young Gibson rode in two races in England in 1961. He came fourth in one race and ninth in the other.

Charley is 19 years old. He said that this chance is what he always wanted and he hopes to make good.

1967

Wednesday, April 19, 1967.

EDITORIAL

No Cause For Despair

By ETIENNE DUPUCH

I HAVE always thought that "yes" and "no" were the most important words in my language. Any person who learns early in life to use these two small words — and stick to a decision — is not likely to be borne down by many serious problems.

But, however clear the path may be, there are dark periods when one is inclined to wonder whether the rewards one may expect out of life are worth the effort that must go into certain positions.

It is here that another small word plays an important part in human experience. That word is "hope". When a situation looks hopelessly bleak we are buoyed up by the hope that there is a silver lining somewhere on the distant cloud.

And usually there is.

That is why Helen Keller, the remarkable blind intellectual, could — in spite of her affliction — say with confidence: "Be not dismayed; in the future lies the Promised Land."

I was busy in my office on Tuesday when the receptionist phoned through to say that a young man wanted to see me. I try not to turn anyone away who comes to see me but I was in no mood at that moment to see anyone.

After a moment's hesitation I told her to send him in.

The door opened to reveal a slim youth of almost 20, trailed by a little boy pealing a length of sugar cane with his teeth.

"I'm Charles Gibson, the champion jockey at the track," he introduced himself, as I held out my hand to greet him.

"I have brought you a cheque for the Crippled Children's Fund," he said, handing me an envelope.

"Who sent it?" I asked.

"It's from me for the children," he said. "I've been the champion jockey at the track for the past four years. For this I receive a bonus of $286 (£100). I've been wanting to do something decent with this money."

"That's very commendable," I said, taking the cheque from the envelope. It was for $100.

"Last year," he told me, "I gave a half to my grandmother and the other half to my uncle who brought me up and has been like a father to me. "This year I'm giving $100 to the Crippled Children's Fund and $100 to the Ranfurly Homes for Children," he told me.

"And the other $86?" I asked. By this time I was really interested in a youngster who was so concerned for the welfare of others.

"I'm giving that to my church, St. Joseph's Church," he said.

Now 20 years of age, he has been riding at the track for seven years, during the last four of which he has been the champion.

But he recognizes the fact that he cannot make riding a career. He must do something else. And so he spends his summers as an apprentice at the Nassau Electric Co.

Another racing season at Nassau's unique Hobby Horse Hall.

225

Opening Day, January 3, 1967

Saturday. January 14, 1967.

Champion jockey Charley Gibson booted home three winners yesterday, including the winner of the featured fifth race, at Hobby Horse Hall.

Yesterday he was in the money every time on six mounts. In addition to his wins, Gibson was second twice and third once.

Above he is shown leading Sea Fury to the wire on Henry Burrows' Mr. B. He also won on Bernese Albury's Mop Young in the second and on Ellen Burrows' Diamond in the fourth.

Brothers Anthony and Charley Gibson are shown parading in front of the Club House before the running of the first race. Anthony is shown on Revenge, No. 1, which replaced Appian Way (scratched). Revenge was fourth. Charley is pictured on Lady Bird, No. 5, which was second to the winner Mr. D., with jockey A. Saunders up.
—Tribune Photo

FULL

FIRST RACE
1. MR. D (2) 31|-, 15|3, 11|
2. LADY BIRD (5) 14|9, 13|
3. INTERROGATOR (4) 15

SECOND RACE
1. CANDY (8) 55|3, 20|3, 16|
2. CUPID (2) 39|-, 22|3
3. WINDY (4) 18|9

Sporting Sam's
three winners

Nostalgia Moments

Noted owner and Breeder of Race Horses Mr. Percival Munnings is seen among his celebrity friends cutting his birthday cake. The next day his pride and joy of his racing stable "Mercy Percy" was killed. L.R. Mr. Sidney Poitier noted Academy Award Movie Star, Golf Professional Mr. "Nine" Rolle, Mr. Munnings, and the Bahamas first Prime Minister Sir Lynden Oscar Pindling.

January 10, 1967, the PLP won the general election after Sir Randol Fawkes of the Labour Party and Sir A. R. Braynen, independent candidate, cast their votes in support of the PLP.

Friday, January 27, 1967

Dancer Shies to Death on Rails

Hobby Horse Hall recorded its first racing tragedy for the season when trainer David Strachan's Southern Dancer had to be shot after shying into the rail in the third race at the seven-furlong post. Jockey J. Anderson, fortunately, was not hurt.

March 1967

HORSE DIES IN HHH MISHAP

By SCOOP

Hobby Horse Hall recorded it second fatal accident to a horse yesterday in the five furlong fifth race feature when Percival Munnings' four years old quarter, Mercy Percy ridden by Leslie Johnson, stumbled into the rail, and was killed. Here are the results of yes-

Horse Dies in HHH Mishap

Hobby Horse Hall recorded its second fatal accident to a horse. In the five-furlong fifth feature race when Percival Munnings's four-year-old Mercy Percy, ridden by Leslie Johnson, stumbled into the rail and a long piece of cedar railing believed to be over one hundred years old was broken into his side. The gallant and courageous stallion continued to run around the racecourse with the cedar plank in his side to the awe of the crowd. Mercy Percy died at the finish line!

April 15, 1967

Go-Billy-Go Is Horse of the Year

Torrid stretch-run from eighth position, owned by Mrs. Vainetta Moss, ridden by George Godet, and trained by Kenneth Glinton.

CHAMPION JOCKEY . . . Charley (Diamond Kid) Gibson is all smiles after winning the top jockey honours for the fourth straight season. Mr. Wenzel Nicolls, chairman of the Racing Commission (left), congratulates the "kid" for his excellent season's efforts. Standing next to Gibson is Mr. Frank Smith, a member of the Racing Commission.

Top Jockey Honors for the Fourth Straight Season

Champion Charlie "Diamond Kid" Gibson was selected as the top jockey of the 1967 racing season, with a record of forty-seven wins, forty-seven seconds, and thirty-five thirds.

Gibson nipped his last season all-time record with forty-six wins. Mr. Wenzell Nicholls, chairman of the Racing Commission, congratulated the "kid" for his excellent effort during the season. Mr. Frank Smith, member of the Racing Commission, also offered congratulations to the young rider.

Jockey Gibson donated his entire check to charity, giving $100 to Ranfurly Home for Children, $100 to the Crippled Children's Fund, and the remaining $80 to St. Joseph Catholic Church.

SCORPIO, the top native horse in the feature race today at H.H.H. proudly held by his groom Nigel Ingraham. The Galedo-Miss Sans stallion will face the starter for the first time this season.

Groom Nigel Ingraham is seen with his favorite stallion, Scorpio, sired by Galedo and Miss San. In the early '60s, Nigel was also a stable boy, and then he became a jockey. Nigel won his first race that he rode on the filly Lady Ann (very few jockeys win on their first mount). He is also known for his famous ride on Cupid. The racing stewards fined Jockey Ingraham for excessively whipping his horse during a one-mile race.

It is also interesting to note that Nigel started as a stable boy and moved up to jockey, groom, assistant racing secretary, and handicapper, racing secretary and handicapper and assistant managing director of Hobby Horse Hall (horse racing industry really provides professional careers).

1968 Racing Season

Owner of the winning horse "Pepsi" was Kay Thompson is all smiles after receiving the Balmoral Beach Hotel Cup Race a top "Pepsi" jockey Austin Saunders, trainer Mr. C. Marchall

One mile of aluminum replaces the 173 years of cedar pine rail. HHH management continue to upgrade the racing facility to ensure the safety of the horses and jockeys.

Ambulance to the Hospital Jockey injured at the finish line

****

April 1, 1968
Hundreds Paid Respects
Jockey Laid To Rest

Hundreds of relatives, students, racing officials, and friends paid their last respect to the late jockey Henry Burrows Jr. at St. Joseph Church, Boyd Road. The students of John F. Kennedy Drive School turned out in almost full numbers in their uniforms, and the jockeys paid their special respect by donning their riding outfits for the sad occasion.

SENATOR THE HON. CLEMENT MAYNARD, right, and
Wenzel Nichols, chairman of the Racing Commission left, and
other members of the commission, judges and stewards are
seen in the procession to the graveside.

Ivan James

THE FAMILY OF THE DEPARTED JOCKEY ... His father, Henry Sr., consoles his aunt Mavis. One of his sisters is seen at left.

Burrows, only fourteen at the time of his untimely death, was one of the younger members of the jockeys who currently ride at the track. He succumbed late Friday night, March 29, after receiving multiple lacerations, broken ribs, and a lacerated liver. The incident occurred during the sixth race of the afternoon when Burrows riding atop Mr. B. was involved in a four-horse spill that sent three other jockeys to the hospital.

In his third season, a happy-go-lucky, energetic youngster, he could rarely be seen with a frown on his face. He always enjoyed a quip with his fellow jockeys and friends.

MORTICIAN Raleigh Butler consoles the grieving mother, Dorothy
Ferguson.

HANDICAPPER HARCOURT BASTIAN, leads Burrows' former in procession.

HANDICAPPER HARCOURT BASTIAN, leads Burrows' former colleagues in procession.

The fifth race of the day, Friday, was the Balmoral Beach Hotel Cup Race that was won by Alfred "Uncle" Glinton on Miss Go Jax. The clerk of scales jokingly jibed Burrows, who was in the process of weighing in for the next race,

> "Henry, I know that you were wishing that it was you and not Uncle who won the cup." He laughingly replied, "It doesn't matter whether I won, because the trophy is going to our house anyhow."

Advantage Taker: Horse of the Year

The legend-to-be, Gary Bain, won his first riding title, champion jockey for 1968.

Owner-Trainer Henry Burrows is all smiles after being presented with the Balmoral Beach Hotel Trophy by the General Manager atop of the winning horse Miss Gojax Alfred Uncle Glinton, B. Richardson Groom.

Noted Trainer "Biddy McGregory holds the bridle of the winning horse "Native Pine" ridden by Gary Bain as racing commission chairman Mr. Wenzel Nichols presents the trophy to the owner Mr. Sherman, "Hard Cat" Martin is the Groom.

Danny "Ducer" Ramsey atop Melvin Godet's "Saratoga"

Gary Bain, Jockey Champion 1968

1969

For the first time in history, the Bahamas recorded its first one million tourist arrival.

GARY BAIN, who has only been riding for three years, took the champion jockey award last season. The 16 year old jockey who rides out of Joe Gamadico's stable collected 36 wins.

Bain's trainer Adwis Hall, seen above, feels certain that his jockey can repeat as champion again.

HARD RIDING JOCKEYS vie for rail positions as the action gets under way at Naasan's Hobby Horse Hall Race Track. Top purse money in excess of $600 makes the competition keen among the riders who are among the racing world's youngest.

DANNY "Ducer" Ramsey, who predicted he will win the Champion Jockey Award this year, is seen on Miracle

Will She Ride?

Nineteen-year-old would-be girl jockey Barbara Jo Rubin is greeted at Nassau International Airport Friday by horse owner George Capron, but it appears that it will be a few more days before she'll get a mount at Hobby Horse Hall.

Reason: She'll have to go through Bahamas Racing Commission licensing route. Barbara Jo was scheduled to race two weeks ago at Miami's Tropical Park but male jockeys wouldn't go along with idea. But Capron, who is ZNS disc jockey, offered her chance to ride his "Jimmy Lee." (See story on Page 9.) — Photo by Bob Thompson.

1969

History in the Making at Hobby Horse Hall
HHH Jockeys Refuse to Ride against Barbara Jo Rubin

The nineteen-year-old jockey who was the subject of a jockey revolt at Miami's Tropical Park Racetrack had permission to ride Stoneland, but thirteen jockeys refused to ride against her and caused a similar storm at Hobby Horse Hall. Barbara Jo arrived in Nassau on 24 January 1969 and was greeted by ZNS disc jockey, George Capron, who invited her to the Bahamas to ride his horse, Jimmy Lee, subject to approval of the Bahamas Racing Commission Licensing Route. Mr. Wenzel Nichols, chairman of the Bahamas Racing Commission, said that Miss Rubin could not ride in Nassau because no application on her behalf had been filed with the commission.

No ride tomorrow for Barbara Jo

AMERICAN girl jockey Barbara Jo Rubin will NOT, after all, be riding at Hobby Horse Hall tomorrow afternoon, it was officially announced this afternoon.

Mr. Wenzel Nicholls, chairman of the Bahamas Racing Commission, said that the 19-year-old Miss Rubin — already stymied by male jockeys' protests against her bid to ride on Florida tracks — cannot ride here tomorrow because no application on her behalf has been filed with the commission.

But, said Mr. Nicholls, the commission would be happy to consider an application from Miss Rubin as soon as it was received. By-laws of the commission state that any jockey taking part in an official race must be licensed.

Mr. Nicholls' statement pointed out that there will be further meetings at HHH next week, on Tuesday and Saturday — the implication being that Miss Rubin would be able to ride then if there has been time for the commission to consider any application from her.

The Ministry of Tourism is especially anxious for Miss Rubin to win her personal battle for female rights in the Bahamas. This week the news of the offer of a mount at HHH has brought a deluge of interest from news agencies, newspapers and television news bureaus around the world.

The Ministry of Tourism is especially anxious for Ms. Rubin to win her personal battle for female rights in the Bahamas. This week, the news of the offer of a mount at HHH has brought a deluge of interest from news agencies, newspapers, and television news bureaus from around the world. Jockeys at Hobby Horse Hall said that they would refuse to ride against Barbara Jo if she would be given permission to compete at the track.

Champion jockey Gary Bain told *Tribune* reporter, the late Wenty Ford, that she shouldn't ride here among the male jockeys, and he wouldn't feel good riding against her. If the jockeys in the USA did not let her ride, we should not let her ride in the Bahamas. Other jockeys had the same opinion (Austin Saunders, Danny Ramsey, Howard Jolly), but Panamanian jockey Victor Rodriquez spoke in favor of her riding. It would be good for the track, he said. Trainer Melvin Godet also spoke in favor of Barbara Jo, "I'm all for it, she can ride a few of my horses," he said.

GIRL JOCKEY Barbara Jo Rubin poses with six of the jockeys who rode in the fourth race on Saturday at Hobby Horse Hall. Miss Rubin was supposed to have ridden in this race but could not because her riding licence was not granted. She will definitely be riding tomorrow in the fourth race. She will be riding Fly Away.

No Ride for Barbara Jo on Saturday

Monday, January 27, 1969
Racing Commission Grants License to Barbara Jo Rubin

STROLLING ALONG   Barbara Jo Rubin is caught by cameraman Bob Thompson strolling to the paddock area along with Racing Commission chairman, Wenzel Nicholls and promoter George Capron, right.

Female jockey Barbara Jo Rubin made history at Hobby Horse Hall yesterday by becoming the first woman jockey to ride at the track and bringing in her mount to first-place finish. Riding Fly Away in the fourth race, five-furlong race distance, Barbara Jo got off to flying lead, which she maintained throughout the race as she headed around the turn into the homestretch. Austin Saunders, riding Sepia, started to close the gap, but a few taps with the whip was all Fly Away needed to finish four lengths ahead of the field. As she rode for the weigh-in, she was congratulated with a kiss by her U.S. trainer, Byron Webber, and handshake from disc jockey George Capron, who was partially responsible for Barbara Jo Rubin riding in Nassau.

CHECKING THE WEIGHT — Thaddeus Wilson checks Barbara's weight, while local trainer Mel Godet looks on. Barbara weighed in at 112 pounds for the ride.

Webber, who seemed overjoyed with his jockey's performance, said, "I think this will open the door for her to ride back home."

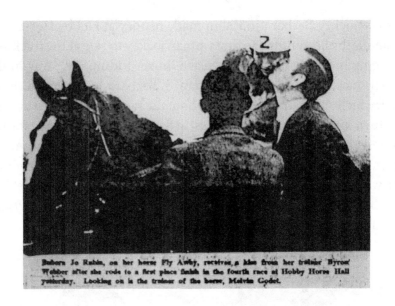

Barbara Jo Rubin, on her horse Fly Away, receives a kiss from her trainer Byron Webber after she rode to a first place finish in the fourth race at Hobby Horse Hall yesterday. Looking on is the trainer of the horse, Melvin Godet.

On February 17, 1969, Diane Crump was the first female jockey licensed in the United States and received her permit from the Hialeah stewards.

DPM Mr. A.D. Hanna presents the Racing Commission Trophy to Mr. Mike Darville owner of the winning Horse "Southern Star" ridden by Tyrone "Buck" Williams, and trained by Mr. Frank Walker.

1969 Riding Champion
Tyrone "Buck" Williams
Horse of the Year: Regal Ranger

(1)   Saul Silberman, owner of Tropical Park in Miami, Florida, purchased the controlling shares in Hobby Horse Hall (Raceco Bahamas Ltd.) from Dr. Raymond Sawyer.

GRANTS TOWN CUP
RACE PRESENTATION –
Miss Ethlyn Taylor presents
owner-trainer   James
Fernander with his trophy
after   Fernander's   Great
Surprise (ridden by Austin
Saunders) won the Grants
Town Cup Race yesterday.
Pictured from left to right
are: Nelson Chipman, owner
of the Bootleggers Inn who
donated the trophy; Miss
Taylor, Hubert Chipman,
John Chipman, Fernander,
Joel Dawkins (groom), Great
Surprise   with   jockey
Saunders,   and   assistant
trainer   Alfred   Adderley
PHOTO: Rickey Wells.

Trainer Wendell "Cray" Williams is seen with his Olympic Stride as "Golden Slipper" crosses the finish line first.

Mr. Neville Smith owner of the winning horse "Golden Slipper" ridden by Buck Williams received the winning trophy as trainer Williams holds the bridle.

Saturday's cup race winner

GOING into the first turn of Saturday's nine-furlong Queen's Cup Race at the Hobby Horse Race Track are: Miss Glo (outside), Hot Tomato (middle) and Annonymous (5). The (No. 4) winner, Una Cupa de Vino is back of Hot Tomato with Austin Saunders aboard BELOW: Pictured (from left) are: Racing Commission chairman Wenzel Nichols, Roy Glass, who accepted the owner's trophy, the Governor, Lord Thurlow, winning trainer Whitfield Demeritte, an unidentified groom and jockey Austin Saunders aboard Una Cupa De Vino (4). PHOTOS: Rickey Wells.

The Britania Beach Hotel and Casino executive' presents the Casino Tray Trophy to the owner of the winning horse "Jet Sam" ridden by Danny Ramsey trained by G. Evans and C. Eneas Groom, Mrs. G. Evans holds the trophy.

(2) Mr. Silberman wants to change the name of HHH to Nassau Racecourse, contending that the jockey club of USA will recognize the racing facility.

(3) International permit for Austin Saunders.

Racing Commission Chairman Mr. Wenzel Nichols and DPM Mr. Arthur Hanna congratulates Jockey Austin Saunders for achieving his International Jockey Licence. L.R. Mr. R. Godet Mr. Wenzel Nichols, D.P.M. Mr. Arthur Hanna and Mr. Sidney Wilson.

Last August, Austin Saunders, along with twenty-nine other Bahamian jockeys, attended riding school in Ocala, Florida, at the Ocala Stud Farm. Because of his performance at the school, his teacher, Bobby Martin, a veteran of over 1,100 races, recommended Saunders for an international license, and shortly before the close of the course, Saunders obtained the license.

HOBBY HORSE HALL - Opening Meetings of the 1970 season are drawing large crowds to HHH. Racing will continue on Tuesdays and Saturdays through April.

Saunders Gets Three Victories at Hobby Horse Hall's Opener

Austin Saunders rode away with three victories, including both halves of the daily double on the opening day of the 1970 racing season. This was not the first time both halves of the daily double were won by the same jockey at Hobby Horse Hall. During the 1948–'49 racing season, Austin's uncle, Sammie "Reverend" Saunders of Just Rite Bakery, was the first jockey to win both halves of the daily double at Hobby Horse Hall Racetrack, riding Second Eleven and Glamour Gal.

The Saunders family of jockeys: Isaac Saunders, Sammie Saunders II, Oswald Saunders, Timothy Saunders, Daniel Saunders, Austin Saunders, Ant. Saunders.

Lady Sassoon is seen presenting the Sir Victor Sassoon Eve Cup to Kenneth "Houly" Seymoure on behalf of Mr. Will Curtis owner of the winning horse Lady Mary. Left to right racing commission member Mr. Godet noted movie actor Robert Mitchum Lady Sassoon, Mr. Saul Silberman owner of Nassau Race Course Hobby Horse Hall, Mr. Wenzel Nichols Chairman Bahamas Racing Commission and Mr. Otis Brown member.

Sir Etienne Dupuch accepts a check donation for charitable organizations in the Bahamas from Mr. Saul Silverman owner of Hobby Horse Hall Race Track.

Day at the Races

Mr. Saul Silberman, Mr. and Mrs. Dawes of Miami Florida is seen at Hobby Horse Hall.

Champion Jockey for 1970, Austin Saunders

**Horse of the Year: Mike Darville's Regal Ranger
Saul Silberman Dies Suddenly in Miami, Florida**

May 1970

Stephen Calder obtained a summer racing permit, then held the first Calder (the first summer Thoroughbred racing meeting in Florida's history) at Tropical Park in Miami, Florida.

for an opening, into a clinch. **PHOTO: Franklyn Ferguson.**

Regal Ranger shows top form

Fatal spill for Miss Eclipse

By LEROY PRATT

...showing the form which twice earned him ...showing staged a strong stretch run to win ...Automobile Dealers Association Cup Race at the ...Race Track Saturday.

ECHO, ridden by Joe Horton heads the field at the first turn during Saturday's Michigan Automobile Dealers Association Cup Race at the Hobby Horse Race Track. Regal Ranger won the race. **PHOTO: RICKEY WELLS.**

Deputy Prime Minister A. D. Hanna is caught by photographer Franklyn Ferguson as he is about to open the racing gate to start the 1971 horse racing season on Saturday.

Name change for Hobby Horse Hall for the second time. Name changed to Hobby Horse Racetrack (HHRT).

1971

ON BEHALF of George Christie, owner of Georgia, Chris Christwell accepts Balmoral Beach Hotel Cup from Mrs. Ivor Petrak, wife of the hotel manager after the victory at the Nassau Race Course on Tuesday. John Bain was the winning jockey, and with the winner are trainer Charles "Porky" Moxey and (right) assistant trainer Harold Jolly. PHOTO Rickey Wells.

Ivan James

A Bahamian profile where ordinary lives become extraordinary.

RACE TRACK PEOPLE....No. 1 in a series

'Cordy' Bastian

Key man at

Hobby Horse

HARCOURT "CORDY" BASTIAN

RACING Secretary and Handkeeper for Hobby Horse Race Track, Harcourt "Cordy" Bastian is dubbed "the man behind the scenes" by his peers because there is no doubt in their minds that he "will get the job done."

Quiet-spoken and graying, the 46 year-old Cordy has a manner that carries a solid ring of authority and self assurance. His face is etched with laughter lines, a result of his wry wit and Bahamian sense of humour.

Cordy believes that the positive key to the future of racing in the Bahamas is the co-operation of horse-owners, trainers, jockeys, management and the racing commission. As the Racing Secretary and Handkeeper there is little doubt that his voice would carry much weight in directing the locl destiny of racing, originally initiated by officers f the British West India Regiment stationed here.

True to adage, "the early bird catches the worm" Cordy whips through a work-day routine that leaves most of his associates breathless and fatigued. His average of 12 hours per day, at the race track, is an indication of his success story. Cordy rises early and is usually the first person at Hobby Horse Race track – and the last to leave.

can be expected . The hardest job is to get the owners and trainers familiarized with new system."

He admits that ant the outset of the 1972 racing season there were a few difficulties, but smiles reassuringly that these have all being ironed out. "by the end of February all houses will be classified alphabetically, thus making the present system more efficient," he said.

Cordy's multiple duties and responsibilities include: the overall security operations on Hobby Horse Race Track, the accumulation of the racing information and scheduling of races and finally maintenance of the stable area.

It was in 1941 that Cordy Bastian was to begin his association with racing. He began as a jockey, and has worked himself up through groom grainer, and regulation officer with the Racing Commission.

OPPORTUNITY

Then in 1967 Cordy Bastian was appointed handkapper under the former weight system or handicapping.

This promotion came after two years as an adviser to the Racing Community.

The opportunity that Cordy had awaited so long was finally to present itself prior to the 1972 racing season. Cordy was named for the prestigious post of Racing Secretary a job which requires experience, determination, persistence and training. For the past summer in preparation for this position at Tropical Park in Florida where he studied the international system of Handicapping. Previously, he had studied operations at Gulf Stream Park.

Proud of his new position, Cordy considers one of his functions to provide continuous training to acquaint horse owners and trainers with the new system. He has been unable to provide as much training to acquaint horse owners and trainers with the new system. He has been unable to provide as much training as he had planned but hopes to intensify this training programme when the season ends.

264

Keith Finley's Chubasco wins Horse of the Year.

Gary Bain, champion jockey with a record of sixty-six wins.

Tourist at Hobby Horse Hall

Queen's Cup race winners.

Minister of Tourism and Communications Clement T. Maynard (left) poses with winners of the Queen's Cup Race after presenting them with their trophies at Nassau Race Course on Saturday. Others (from left) are: owner Charles Minns, trainer Densal Munnings, jockey Gary Bain (atop the cup winner, La Negra Fueta), Gladstone Scavella and, racing Commission chairman, Wenzel Nichols. The Queen's Cup race, run earlier in the season, was won by Minns five year old mare, but the presentation was delayed until Saturday.

Wendell Williams, leading trainer.

Victor Claridge's Count Zorich out of the Countess. Pie Maker was the two-year-old Bahamian Thoroughbred champion.

Victor Claridge "Count Zorich" with a burst of speed around the two furlong bend champion two year old for 1971.

BAHAMIAN BROOD MARES IN foal
KENTUCKY DERBY POTENTIAL'S?

Harcourt Bastian was appointed racing secretary and handicapper
for the 1972 racing season.

CUP WINNER—Sun Tiger, with whip-holding jockey Anthony Saunders sitting aboard, captured the Bahamas Printing and Litho Co. Cup Race last Tuesday afternoon during the 22nd meet at the Hobby Horse Race Track. From left to right for the presentations are groom Alexander Forbes, trainer Dudley Lewis, jockey Saunders, handler Prince Hepburn, Mrs. Enid Lewis who accepted the trophy on behalf of owner Jenson Taylor, Mrs. Farrington, Bahamas Printing Co. owner Mr. Paul Farrington and HHRT handicapper Nigel Ingraham.

★ ★ ★ ★ ★ ★ ★ ★

June's Joy Wins Cup

Quinella Pays $685.35

Livingston Bostwick presents Hector Smith owner of "Miss Millie" the winning horse, the Ambassador Beach Hotel trophy jockey K. Johns and Advis Hall trainer, and Mr. Ivan James Sales and Director.

Former Prime Minister of the Bahamas Sir Lynden Oscar Pindling and Sir Milo B. Butler first Governor General of the Bahamas were guest speakers at the Bahamas Race Horse Owners Associations monthly meeting at Britley's Restaurant and bar, is seen playing a game of pool while Mr. Wellington Ferguson president of B.R.H.O.A looks on intently.

Lady Marguerette Pindling with her charming smile looks on as Sir Lynden make the winning shot!

President Wellington Ferguson is seen with L. Mr. Ellie Rolle noted
trainer and Mr. W. Williams after the monthly BRHDA meeting at
Britley's.

SWINGING into the home stretch, Lady Archibold (6) leads the field, followed closely by Selim Fathalla (4) and coming strongly on the outside is the winning horse, Chubasco. This was the action in the second race on Saturday. PHOTO: Rickey Wells.

DPM Arthur D. Hanna presents the Bahamas Racing Commission most prestigious trophy for two years olds Bahamian bred to Mr. Mike Darville,

The noted American horse trainer and breeder Mr. Oscar Dishman was the guest of Mr. Wenzel Nichols chairman of the Bahamas Racing Commission, holds the winning horse: Jackie". Mr. Dishman is also the trainer and breeder for the noted Bahamians Dr. Archie Donaldson and his brother Dr. Elwood Donaldson. "Silver Series" Golden Don, "Dondigold" were World Class Race Horses. "Silver Series" in 1978 Race competitively with "Alydar" and the Last Triple Crown Champion "Affirmed" in thirty five years! Dondigold and Golden Don were turf specialist in company with the great "Forego".

Mr. Richard Wright far right and family enjoy a day at the races at Hobby Horse Hall.

1972
by Leroy Pratt

Bahamas Racehorse Owners Association
boycott for increased purses.

Bahamas Racing Commission Chairman Wenzel Nichols and guest among the enthusiastic racing fans at the Hobby Horse Hall.

Prime Minister Cup Presentation

Sidney Wilson, Roosy Godet, Assistant Groom and Assistant Trainer, Mr. Elliston Rolle, Trainer holding the Prime Minister's Cup and Sir Lynden Pindling Prime Minister and Racing Commission members.

Fantastic Run
April 8, 1972

Prime Minister Sir Lynden Oscar Pindling presents
Jockey John Bain his trophy after winning The Prime
Minister's Cup Race aboard Reina De Wyon owned by
Miss Cynthia Rolle and trained by Mr. Elliston Rolle.

Days at the Races.

"Thank you for coming, sir," says track owner, Jimmie Silberman, to deputy prime minister, A. D. Hanna, who started the first race of the 1972 racing season.

Champion jockey, Bain, starts season with two winners.

The Tribune

DOWN the back stretch in Saturday's fifth race, La Ebony (9) with Kevin Johnson aboard leads D'Assinator (4) with Stan McNeil in the saddle by a half stride. McNeil guided home his mount, ahead of Fantasma (3) to pay the day's highest of $254.30. PHOTO: Rickey Wells.

Jockey dispute delays race track meet

By LEROY PRATT

THE JOCKEYS at the Hobby Horse Race Track held up Saturday's meet by a little over half an hour when they staged a wildcat strike in protest of the $3 each jockey received for a mount.

In an almost unbelievable ride, Bain won the native-bred Three-Year-Old BRC Cup Race aboard the Orange Hill stable's Patches, and the native Thoroughbred––two-horse race––three-year-old BRC Cup Race atop Victor Claridge's Count Zorich.

Tuesday, April 11, 1972

RING OF FIRE (inside), with Harry Hinds up, leads the field at the top of the stretch during yesterday's sixth race. Challenging Hinds on the outside is Eugene Stirrup and Yellow Elder (3). PHOTO: Rickey Wells.

Griffiths rides 7 winners over the holiday meets

--CHAMPION BAIN'S FANTASTIC RUN

By LE ROY PRATT

JOCKEY GEOFFREY GRIFFITH turned out the top rider in the Hobby Horse Race Track 'ong holiday weekend meets Saturday and Monday by riding home seven winners.

The 26-year-old Barbadian jockey won two races on Saturday and yesterday brought five first place finishers across the finish line. Griffith also added a pair of seconds and thirds to his two-day effort in the saddle.

Another IHRT rider, Michael Brown, managed four wins a second and three thirds out of Saturday and yesterday's meet. A first year man, Brown, as a result, moved up from fourth to third spot in this season's jockey race. The four wins gave the 17-year-old

John began running again. At the bottom of the back stretch, Bain had caught Rango's Image (2) and Neysa's Joy (3) and was heading for the rest of the field of three horses – Nado's Child (1), Winged Dutchess (6) and Jungle Pie (4).

At the two-furlong turn, Bain had already taken over second place and was heading for the front running Nado's Child, ridden by Austin Saunders. At the one furlong pole Bain took over the race to win going away.

EASTER MONDAY'S RESULTS

HERE ARE the results of yesterday's Easter Monday holiday Hobby Horse Race Track meet:
FIRST RACE – 6 furs. 1. Chime Song (6) – G. Griffith – $13.80, ...

EIGHTH RACE – 4½ furs. 1. Wild Fire (4) – H. Fernandez – $136.30, $12.85, $5.20; 2. Red Suit (5) – A. Saunders – $5.80, $3.45 3. Mea Constance (3) – G. Griffith ...

DRUMBEAT CUP WINNER, Fantasma (4) ridden by champion jockey Gary Bain, puts the nose on La Ebony (9) and Austin Saunders at the finish. PHOTO: Rickey Wells.

Griffiths rides seven winners over the Easter holiday meets.

Very successful 1972 season.

Champion Gary Bain closes out track season with sixty-three winners.

GO-GO-GIRL all set to go January 2, when the gates of Hobby Horse Race Track opens for the 1973 race season, is seen in an exercise with trainer George Christie and Jockey Michael Brown who rode the mare to three victories in the 1972 season.

Hobby Horse Race Track To Open January 2

They're off! To start the 1973 racing season at
Hobby Horse Hall (Photo by Ricky Wells)

Track win meant $1,000 to a horse owner, says Manager Kemp. Despite a preseason threat from the horse owners not to run their horses, the Hobby Horse Racetrack, still managed a very successful season, according to the track's general manager, Garth Kemp.

Mr. Arthur Nairn the Phantom is being dressed before a race.

Count Zorich voted Horse of the Year 1972.

1973

(1)   Glen Holmes, racing secretary and handicapper.
(2)   Ribbon cutting ceremony at the opening of Hobby Horse Racetrack.

RECEPTION—The stars of "The Fergusons of Farm Road," a weekly Radio Bahamas production, were feted at a reception given in their honour by the Ministry of Tourism at the Sheraton-British Colonial Hotel on Tuesday evening. Pictured left to right are: S.N. Chib, Director of Tourism; Miss Pandora Gibson, who played the role of Gladys; Kenneth Wild of FINCO; the Minister of Tourism, the Hon. Clement T. Maynard; Mrs Learlene Collie (Miss Lye—the most popular personality on the show); Greg Lampkin (George) and producer Carl Bribel of Radio Bahamas.

'Fergusons Of Farm Road' Cast Gets Tourism Ministry Treat

"The Fergusons of Farm Road," the Bahamas' first radio soap opera underlying the theme of tourism, has come to an end. Written by Jeanne Thompson, the show ran for 132 weeks and was sponsored by the Ministry of Tourism and Finance Corporation of Bahamas as an adjunct to the nationwide "Friendliness Through Understanding" campaign launched on 29th March, 1976.

Although the active campaign is no longer in effect, "The Fergusons" continued the underlying theme of the campaign, courtesy, friendliness, good service and an overall amicable attitude toward the tourists who come to our shores. Participants of the weekly Radio Bahamas production were feted Tuesday evening (January 2) at a reception given by the Ministry of Tourism at the Sheraton-British Colonial Hotel.

Minister of Tourism, Clement T. Maynard, personally thanked those present for their participation in the programme. He said "The Fergusons" had done an "excellent job" in furthering the basic ideas of tourism.

"The message of good service, courtesy and making people happy by letting them know you care, was meaningfully and delightfully conveyed through characters Bahamians can identify with," Mr. Maynard said.

The Minister indicated that discontinuance of the programme had nothing to do with the quality of the serial or the script. "The programme," he said, "had delivered the message of tourism and for the time being, had come to an end."

Other radio features of the "Friendliness Through Understanding" campaign of a shorter duration than "The Fergusons" were several more vignettes called "One In A Million" and narrated by Bahamian actor Sidney Poitier.

A Radio Bahamas Production by Carl Bethel, "The Fergusons of Farm Road" was heard each Wednesday at 7:45 p.m. The final episode was heard December 27 when the characters bid farewell to each other and listeners.

Actors in the Ferguson family are: Zeke Ferguson (Charles Rowley), his wife Mina (Miriam Johnson) and their children, Samuel (Eddie Minnis), Ormel (Teddy Grant), Earl (Tommy Thompson) and Blossom (Heather Thompson). Others are the cantankerous Miss Lye (Learlene Collie) and her Pretty Boy (Martin Lundy), sister Gladys (Pandora Gibson), and her daughter Janet (Rhonda Grant). Also the Bishop (Calvin Cooper) and Miss Suzy (Erma Albury).

(3) January 5, the most popular Bahamian soap opera, *The Ferguson's of Farm Road*, ends (no more Ms. Lye).

(4) Jimmy Silberman, owner of HHRT, dies suddenly in Miami, Florida.

(5) Hobby Horse Racetrack not for sale, says Mrs. Silberman.

(6) William Dawes, lawyer for Mrs. Silberman, to take control of the racetrack.

(7) Jockey Gary Bain won four races.

(8) Winston Knowles's Lolipop ridden by Gary Bain won the Racing Commission Three-Year-Old Cup Race.

(9) Racehorse Jubils was suspended from racing by the stewards, needs more training.

(10) Horan Shoran won Horse of the Year for 1973.

(11) Gary "Messiah" Bain won his fourth riding title with fifty-six wins.

(12) For the first time in the history of HHRT, the racing stewards did not honor the leading jockey. They contended that Jockey Bain drew a suspension earlier in the season for indifferent riding.

(13) Melvin Godet voted top trainer for 1973. Larry Demeritte was second.

The Bahamas Hotel Corporation was established to regulate the operations of the mentioned hotels. The following is the story that must be told for future generations for them to know.

The PLP won the 1968 general election by a landslide, and local and foreign investors saw a continuance of stability in the Bahamas. General Bahamian Co. decided to build a four hundred–room hotel on Cable Beach and gave the manager's contract to the largest hotel chain in the world, Sonesta Hotels, owned and operated by the Sonnabend brothers. Mr. Robert Symonette, CEO, GBC; Mr. David Johnson, president; Mr. Bismarck Coakley, VP; and Bradley Roberts, SVP, became officers of the General Bahamian Company.

(1) Holiday Inn: 550 rooms on Paradise Island.

(2) Mr. Charles Wohlstetter, CEO of Hemisphere Hotels, New York City, constructed a three-hundred-room hotel in Coral Harbour, next door to the world-famous Coral Harbour Hotel and Golf Club and Marina, owned and operated by Mr. Lindsay Hopkins and his sister, Mrs. Sally McKillips. It is also interesting to note that Mr. Hopkins owned the Carl G. Fisher Corporation that developed the world-famous Miami Beach. Geographically, it was perfect for New Providence as it was an economic boom for the construction workers in New Providence.

In 1969, the New York stock exchange crashed, and it created a major cash flow problem for Hemisphere Hotels Development. Hemisphere Hotels Coral Harbour Project came to a complete stop in 1970 with an 80 percent completion. In 1971, the Coral Harbour Hotel closed its doors!

Sonesta and the Holiday Inn chain survived, and the Sonesta and Holiday Inn Hotel opened on schedule in 1971.

In 1973, Mr. Robert Symonette, CEO of GBC, agreed to sell the Sonesta Beach Hotel to Mr. Ward of Toronto, Canada, owner of Wardair Airlines, one of the world's largest privately owned airlines. All parties agreed in principal subject to government approval. In his application for work permits, he wanted a total number of 110–120 work permits for his people. The total Bahamian staff consisted of 240. The prime minister, Lynden Oscar Pindling, told Mr. Ward that his request was not in the best interest of the Bahamian people. ("Your request is denied!") Executives of Sonesta and the GBC executives were temporarily disappointed because the sale of the hotel was not completed at that time. Prime Minister Pindling, being pragmatic, realized the position of the Local Investment Co. (GBC), presented them a check for the sale of the hotel, and it is interesting to note that the Emerald Beach Hotel was up for sale and the Balmoral Beach Hotel. The Bahamas government purchased both hotels to sustain the jobs of over eight hundred Bahamian hotel workers, and Mr. Robert Souers was appointed CEO and managing director of all government-owned hotels by the Hotel Corporation of the Bahamas. It was also interesting to note that Mr. Robert Souers's name alone gave the government hotels credit to operate. The government did not supply operational funds.

Many years later, a special group wanted the former prime minister Pindling and DPM, Mr. A. D. Hanna, to endorse the lifting of 15 percent automatic gratuity. He told them that it was very ludicrous for them to make such a suggestion. He told them that 15 percent is over-the-hill money. The love and compassion for the people of the Bahamas, the former prime minister, and the DPM expressed throughout their political career will be second to none!

Debi Noses Out Charity Cup Race

Mr. Garth Kemp, General Manager of H.H.H. presents
Mr. Edmond Lewis, owner of the winning horse
Debi that won the charity cup race. Dudly Lewis
trainer ridden by Jockey Glen Searchwell.

CHAMPIONSHIP JOCKEY GARY BAIN ATOP HORSE OF THE
YEAR Mr. Brite pose with trainer Cecil Rolle and owner Wellington
Ferguson. Miss Nassau High School Ann-Marie Smith is shown
presenting Ferguson with the owner's award. Pictured from left are Mr.
Garth Kemp, general manager of Bahamas Raceco and Mrs. Wellington
Ferguson. Mr. Nigel Ingraham, a Raceco official, stands at right.

1974

(1)   Bahamas Racing Commission chairman Franklyn Wilson says horse racing is a boost to the economy.

Deputy Prime Minister Mr. A.D. Hanna cuts the ribbon for the opening of the 1974 racing season. L.R. Mr. Franklyn Wilson, newly appointed Racing Commission Chairman, DPM Mr. Hanna, Joe Sweeting, Mr. Otis Brown, Sidney Wilson, Mr. Ferguson members of the Racing Commission.

"Crow Dancer" set a fast Pace Heading for the first turn during the Prime Minister Cup Race with H. Hinds in the Iron's.

"Count Zorich" all alone by 16 lengths at the finish.

"COUNT ZORICH"

Austin Saunders displays his classic jockey dismount.

Chairman Franklyn Wilson, Brian Snow, Mr. Claridge, Jockey Saunders and Trainer Melvin Godet.

Victor Claridge count "Zorich" won the Prime Ministers Cup Race ridden by Austin Saunders and Melvin Godet was the trainer.

Sir Lynden Pindling presents the Prime Minister Cup to Austin
Saunders the jockey. Mr. Franklyn Wilson the Racing Commission
Chairman and Melvin Godet looks on.

"COUNT ZORICH"

1975

(1) Mr. Mario Parotti is appointed general manager of Hobby Horse Racetrack.

(2) Mr. Nigel Ingraham, the new racing secretary and handicapper.

(3) Hobby Horse Racetrack opens to a record four thousand racing fans!

HHRT Opens With Exciting Programme

Cuts Ribbon - Beryl Hanna wife of the Deputy Prime Minister Arthur D. Hanna, pictured at right is seen cutting the ribbon to officially open the 1975 Hobby Horse Race Track Season yesterday, while Mario Parotti, General Manager at the track looks on.

(1) Gary "Messiah" Bain won his fifth riding title.
(2) Wellington "Britely" Ferguson, owner of Mr. Brite, sired by amazing Retosada, Horse of the Year for 1974.

Mrs. "Brite"

In true winning form by six.

Trainer George Greenslade walks "Mrs. Brite" to the winners circle
with Stan McNeil the jockey.

Governor General Sir Milo B. Butler and Lady Butler congratulated Jockey Stan McNeil for winning the Governor's Cup on Wellington "Britley" Ferguson. "Mrs. Brite" was trained by George Greenslade. Mrs. Ernestine Dean looks on pensively.

FOUR-year old Shantel owned by Ms. Delores Bowe and ridden by jockey Nelson Sweeting, won the Appleton Cup Race and added purse on Saturday during the 22nd meet of Hobby Horse Race track. Mr. Wendall Lightbourne, a representative of the William Brewer Company sponsors of the Appleton Cup Race presented Ms. Bowe with the huge trophy. Pictured during the presentation: (l. to r.) Crofton Ellis, assistant trainer; Sweeting aboard Shantel; unidentified groom; Mr. Lightbourne; Ms. Bowe owner of Shantel; Nigel "Soup" Ingraham, asst. Managing Director of NRA; and Michael Symonette. PHOTO: Tyrone O'Lander.

Mr. Vivian Thompson is a proud recipient of the Brittania Beach Hotel and Casino Tray Trophy owner of the winning horse "King Fire".

1976

Harcourt "Cordy" Bastian, the new general manager of Hobby Horse Racetrack.

It was in 1940 that Cordy Bastian was to begin his association with racing. He began as a jockey in 1940 and has worked himself through groom, trainer, and regulation officer with the Racing Commission, handicapper, racing public relations officer, racing secretary, and handicapper. He is the key man at Hobby Horse Racetrack (horse racing continues to produce very good characters).

January 9, 1976

The introduction of a new racing system sparked ill feeling among trainers and owners of horses.

The trainers and owners claimed that the new raffle system was unfair and immediately threatened to boycott racing if the system was introduced.

Bahamas Race Horse Owners Association President Mr. Wellington "Britley" Ferguson talks to reporter Gladstone Thurston as "Respect Toy" Bastian looks on intently.

Stan McNeil steers Wheel of Fortune to an easy win over Miss Reward to win Saturday's Governor General's cup race.

Saturday, March 6

Final Season for Hobby Horse Track
Hotel and Casino Complex to be Built

The startling announcement was made today by Racing Commission chairman Franklyn Wilson, but Mr. Wilson assured fans that horse racing will continue next year despite closure of the track. The late Gene Barrett, a top government hotel official, said that hotel management had been told that the complex would open on Cable Beach in the area of the track by 1978 or early 1979.

This, therefore, will be the last racing season at Hobby Horse Racetrack, says Mr. Wilson. However, once plans for the new track have been completed, I feel racing will become bigger here. A new track will mean better horses, better facilities, and bigger bettors!

The future of racing here is very promising. For example, horse breeders in Central Florida have plans to breed top-class horses at Andros, where the conditions are ideal with plenty of grass, land, and water.

Raceco Ltd. has run the track for the past five years and still has two more years of its lease for the track. The company was headed by the late Bill Dawes, a lawyer in Coral Gables, Florida.

Sunday, March 14, 1976

Basil "Duren" Hall, Schlitz Beer's ace, pitches the first perfect game in the history of the Bahamas Baseball Association, blanking Del Jane 5–0.

April 10, 1976

Unheralded Jockey Guides Jengo to
Victory in Bahamas Derby
Derby Day

Mr. Wellington Ferguson is seen fully regale on Bahamas Derby Day at Hobby Horse Hall Race Track.

Unheralded jockey Darius Thompson made his presence known and felt Saturday as he took Jengo and outrode defending champion jockey, Gary "Messiah" Bain, who rode Chutero to win the Bahamas Derby.

Hocus Pocus and Bon Bah Rose carried the pace for the nine-furlong journey until they headed into the far turn where Chutero started to make her bid and move ahead of the field, coming into the homestretch. It was Chutero still holding the lead, followed by Derg and Jengo, who were coming on strong. As the horses approached the one-furlong pole, Jockey Thompson pushed Jengo ahead of Chutero and held his own to the finish line.

DERBY WINNERS — In Derby photos clockwise, from bottom, Joe Sweeting, a member of the Bahamas Racing Commission, presents the Commission trophy to Bertram "Cowboy" Musgrove, left, trainer of the Derby winning horse, Jengo, and winning jockey, Darius Thompson. In second photo, Emerald Glinton presents the Gold and Silversmith floating trophy to owner of Jengo, Stanley Alleyne, while Franklyn Wilson, Chairman of the BRC, looks on. In top photo, Thompson, atop Jengo, (No. 5), takes the lead over Chutterro, partly hidden, as the horses headed down the homestretch and to the finish line. Derg, (No. 8), gives chase. In right photo, Otis Brown, a member of the Commission, presents Musgrove with trophy for being the trainer of Jengo, the Derby winner.

Thompson, on his return to the weigh-in area, was greeted with a thunderous applause from the thousands of horse racing fans who turned out to witness the Bahamas Derby, the first since 1933.

Bain, on his return to the weigh-in, lodged a protest against Thompson, claiming that Jockey Thompson rode him to the rail, causing him to slow down Chutero. After a lengthy observation, the stewards overruled the protests. Jengo was sired by No Seats John-

Sepia, owned by Stanley Alleyne, and trained by Bertram "Cowboy" Musgrove.

Darius "Jockey" Thompson atop "Jengo" is led to the winning circle by his groom.

Mr. Stanely Alleyne owner of "Jengo" is all smiles as trainer Cowboy Musgrove, and Jockey Darius Thompson holds the winning Trophy L.R Mr. Alleyne, Cowboy Musgrove Mr. Joe Sweeting Jockey Thompson and Bahamas Racing Commission Chairman Mr. Franklyn Wilson.

Two Records Set
Saturday, April 10

Danny "the Professional" Ramsey set two records Saturday when he rode Sir Mark, sired by Rainy Lake and Shillalah, in the nine-furlong fourth race and Langton Hilton's Baggers Delight in the five-furlong seventh race. Ramsey rode Sir Mark to a 1.56.3 to break the old mark of 1.59, which was set by Moon Walk and Victor Claridge's Count Zorich.

In the five-furlong seventh race, Ramsey carried Baggers Delight on top of the field from the crack of the gate and pushed her across the finish line in a time of 1.01, breaking the old mark of 1.06.

The boastful Ramsey said confidently after the race that Baggers Delight is the second best horse at the track. Sir Mark is no. 1.

It is also interesting to note that Langton Hilton's Baggers Delight was shipped to Miami's Calder's Racetrack during the summer, and in her first race at the Calder, she was ridden by our very own Austin Saunders. She ran last. Harry Benson was the trainer. Baggers Delight atoned herself and won under the guidance of Gene St. Leon at Hialeah Park, a six-furlong race in 1.10 flat. (The first time in history a horse raced at Hobby Horse Hall Racetrack won a race on the international racing circuit.)

Danny Ramsey's pride stallion, Sir Mark, drops dead after the finish line on closing day. Sir Mark was Horse of the Year 1976.

Nine jockeys were suspended for unsavory practices by the racing stewards.

Gary "Messiah" Bain became champion jockey for the seventh time!

Larry Demeritte was 1976 leading trainer.

King Fire Wins Prime Minister Cup Race

Owner, Russ Thompson, ridden by A. Green, Vivian Thompson, trainer.

(1) Racing stewards suspends six top jockeys.
(2) Racetrack sold to Bahamian group. Mr. George McKinney, president of Nassau Racing Association (NRA).
(3) Mr. Arthur Colebrook, local architect, was appointed general manager of HHRT.

The "Gary Bain" Story

Gary Bain

Gary Bain, the son of Mr. Wilber "Bug" and Doral Bain of Augusta Street, Nassau, Bahamas began his riding career at The Hobby Horse Hall Race Track in 1967, under the guidance of Advis Hall a Young and promising trainer. His potential as a super jockey was evident from the start.

His ability and courage in the handling of horses caught the eye of several trainers, and during the 1968 racing season at Hobby Horse Hall race track, Gary was getting mounts from all of them and proving to be a success. He won his first riding championship title in 1968. The late Buck Williams was the riding champion in 1969 and the laate Austin Saunders in 1970. Gary primed himself and won the riding championship Title for the next six years (71, 72, 73, 74, 75, 76,) in the history of horse racing in the Bahamas, no other jockey won the riding championship title six years consecutively. The late Alfred "Uncle" Glinton won four consecutive titles in 1938, 1939, 1940, 1941, and Charlie "Diamond Kid" Gibson in 1964, 1965, 1966, and 1967. Gary did not ride during the 1977 racing season at Hobby Horse Hall Race Track as that was the year the track CLOSED for good. A noted Bahamian businessman and horseman in The Bahamas, was the main source behind Gary's international riding career. Due to his vast racing network, the Bahamian businessman introduced Gary to his Florida connection, and in 1978 Gary's international riding career began.

Gary was noted to be a master reinsman for two-year-olds in training.

Gary was the exercise Jockey for two well known Bahamian Doctors racing stables with the late Oscar Dishman as their trainer. Gary never rode any of the Doctors horses in races.

Gary won most of his early races on horses owned by the following Bahamian horsemen: the late Mr Philip Pinder, a noted Bahamian Lawyer, Langton Hilton, Tom Ferguson, and twenty five years later in 2003, on horses owned by Mr Theophilis Fritz. It is also interesting to note that "Baggers Delight" and "Pack Buster" were the first products of Hobby Horse Hall Race Track to race at tracks, in North America; "Baggers Delight" at Calder and "Pack Buster" at Suffolk Downs in Boston, MA. In 1983 two promising 2-year-olds racing at Calder were Harold Rose "Rexon's Hope" and MY G.P., Gary Bain was the regular ride for both horses. The Florida stallion stake races for colts were, Dr Fager Division, Affirmed Division, and the In-Reality Division, MY G.P. ran third in the Dr Fager Division with Gary Bain in the Irons, the distance was six furlongs. The In-Reality was the last race of the series 1 1/16 miles Gary selected to ride MY G.P. over Raxon's

Hope not knowing the In-Reality will be split in two division, MY G.P. ran in the first divsion and the Legendary Harold Rose selected Robert Gafflione to ride Rexon's Hope in the second division. MY G.P. won the first division. It was Gary Bain's first major stake race internationally $90,000 purse. Robert Gafflione won on Rexon's Hope in the second division. MY G.P. encounter problems and Rexon's Hope ran in the 1984 Kentucky Derby with Robert Gafflione in the Irons.

(Gary Bain lost the historical Kentucky Derby Mount of his career). In the mid 80's mounts were difficult to obtain, so Gary moved his tack to Detroit Race Course (DRC) Gary became an immediate riding sensation among the top jockeys like Lester Knight, Euclides Vergara, Scott Speith, Danny Scocca to name a few at DRC. Gary won the riding championship title in 1987 at DRC. For the next five years, Gary was also a wizard on the basketball court, in softball and he plays a good game of pool, among the jockeys. It was noted that a group of Bahamian racing fans, Bummy Albury, Nigel Ingraham the late "Fats" Holmes. The Gonzalez Brothers, Dake and Gurth (Salad), Donald Darville, Edmund Lewis, E.J., Walter "Rim" Curtis, William Curtis, the late Jimmy Virgil and yours truly Ivan James attended the races annually, during the summer racing season at DRC and in 1990 the Bahamian knowledge and expertise in horse racing was expressed for the first time internationally. Nigel Ingraham, former Racing Secretary and Assistant General Manager at Hobby Horse Hall Race Track, was invited to be on Scott McGee Breakfast Show at DRC.

In 1991 Ivan James was the guest speaker and Scott McGee Breakfast Show attained its highest rating ever with the appearanced of Nigel Ingraham and Ivan "Abaco" James. The racing fans at DRC were told that whenever a casino opens in Detroit, Detroit Race Course will close! DRC closed after the 1998 racing season.

Gary took his tack back to South Florida in 1992. Noted trainers like Nathan Kelly, Legendary Harold Rose, Fred Warren and Michael Trivigno conintued to use Gary as their regular jockey. Gary got the first call on of Harold Rose's and Nathan Kelly horses.

In April of 1996 Michael Trivigno's promising two-year-old Hoot Coyote Hoot Dominate the Florida two-year-olds w/ Gary Bain in the Irons. Mr Michael Trivigno entered Hoot Coyote Hoot in one of the prestigious two-year-old's races in North America on Kentucky Derby Day, May 4th, 1996 at Churchill Downs in Louisville Kentucky with his regular rider Gary Bain. It was the WHAS TV 89,000 Dollars Stake Race 5 Furlongs Sprint, it was the third race on the Kentucky Derby Day Race program. "Hoot Coyote Hoot won the race and Gary Bain became the first black jockey to win a major stake race on Kentucky Derby Day at Churchill Downs Race Track in 100 years, to the cheers of 142,668 racing fans (the 9th largest attendance in Derby history) including the assemblage of Corporate America and the Bahamian entourage of Ivan "Abaco" James, Earl Fountain, Jermiah Gray and Larry Demeritte who trained horses at Keenanland and Churchill Downs Race Track and Larry is also a breeder of horses in Louisville Kentucky. Larry Demeritte another proud product of Hobby Horse Hall Race Track where ordinary lives become extraordinary lives.

Gary had two mounts on Derby Day he got a 1 st and 2nd, the last black jockey to win a stake race on Derby Day was Jimmy Winkfield who won the Kentucky Derby in 1902 on "Alan a Dale". Jimmy Winkfield was also the second black jockey to win back to back Kentucky Derby's. He won on "His Eminence" in 1901. Isaac Murphy was the first in 1890 - 1891, Jimmy Winkfield lost the 1903 Kenturky Derby on the favourite "Early". Jimmy Winkfield would have been the only jockey in racing history to win the Kentucky Derby in three consecutive years (1901, 1902, 1903).

Gary Bain's international riding career stats in North America and the Caribbean not including the Bahmas in 25 years 1978 - 2003: Mounts 13,030, wins 1039, seconds 1,150, thirds 1,294, 26.9% in the total money earned $9,682,401.

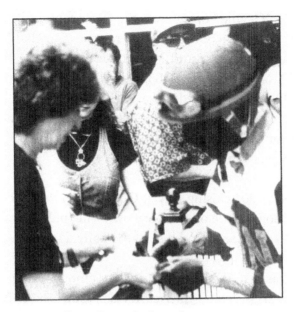

Gary Bain before the race.

Gary Bain and the Chinese Master, George Hosang from Jamaica, endevoured and more successful riding careers in the United States of America and Canada than any other West Indian Jockeys. Gary Bain's lifetime endevours in the field of thoroughbred horse racing has embodied excellence, innovation, leadership unparalleled achievement.

It is also interesting to note that in 1999, Winston Griffith the all-time leading jockey in Jamaica, acquired National Honours. He received the order of Distinction (O.D.) Officer Class from the Jamaican Government. It is also interesting to note that whenever I have a dialogue with one of Gary Bain's admired fans, the former Governor General of The Bahamas, Sir Orville Turnquest, he would ascertain Gary's progress on the international racing circuit and would remind me that whenever Gary comes home on a visit I should bring him to Government House. Gary has not returned home in three years, but has promised to join us for our July 10th celebrations. Gary has had his ups and downs like Lafit Pincay, but he has atoned himself, and most recently at Gulf Stream Park on March 22nd, 2003, he won whilst riding "Orville Forest" over the world famous Jerry Bailey in a 6-furlong sprint $36,000 allowance race at 15-1, "Ballistic Missle" 2nd with Gary Boulanger and Mukhtaser 3rd with the Master Jerry Bailey at 7-2, on March 30th, 2003. He out-duelled the notable Edgar Prado, on 43 to 1. Whoneedsafive, ALL LINE 5-2 with Prado. ALL LINE w/Prado and Whoneedsafive w/Bain was head and head from the one furlong pole to the finish line. Gary's masterful hands and timing won over Prado.

On April 24th, 2003 closing Day at Gulf Stream Park, he displayed a masterful Boogalo ride on our very own Theophlis Fritz's. AMZAC (ANZAC) to win the second half of the daily double.

Gary Bain has sustained his riding career among the top jockey's for the past 25 years in North America. It is so proud to be a BAHAMIAN.

Recognition for your unparalled riding skills for over the past 36 years will not be forgotten. Gary "The Messiah Bain", RIDE ON! RIDE ON! A LIVING LEGEND IN HORSE RACING.

This short biography of Gary Bain has no self enrichment values, it was done solely for the love of our first national sport (Horse Racing), written knowledge, and a tribute to our forgotten hero.

(FOR YOU TO KNOW)

IVAN "ABACO" JAMES

PROUD TO BE A
BAHAMIAN
A Hero's Tribute
To Gary Bain A Proud Product Of
Hobby Horse Hall Race Track
Where Ordinary Lives Become Extraordinary Lives!

Gary "The Messiah" Bain at the Churchill Downs Race Track in Louisville Kentucky, May 4, 1996.

Gary Bain in demand for autographs.

Gary Bain signing autographs for racing fans at Churchill Downs Race Track on Kentucky Derby Day.

Gary Bain accepts Ivan James pre race advice to maintain his mental toughness.

OUR "BAHAMIAN JOCKEY" HERO

MAY 4TH, 1996 - GARY BAIN

The Only Black Jockey In Racing History To Win A Major Stake Race at Churchill Downs Race Track On Kentucky Derby Day To The Cheers Of 142,668 Racing Fans Including The Assemblage of Corporate America in 100 years

The Bahamian
Connection

The Bahamian
Connection

Gary Bain is seen with the Bahamian entourage after winning the WHAS TV most prestigious stake race for two years old.

To the throng of 142,668 racing fans at Churchill downs on Kentucky Derby day May 4th, 1996.

Mr. Larry Demeritte noted Bahamian breeder and trainer of race horses share a special hand shake from Mr. Earl Fountain. It is also interesting to note that in 1983 at Churchill Down Race Track Larry's wife's horse "Lady Sabrina" ridden by one of the worlds famous "jockey" Mr. Pat Day, won a six (6) furlong race, sporting the silk colors of the Bahamian flag.

1977

January 6

(1) Racing Commission rejects peace formula.

(2) The horse owners had threatened to boycott the new season due to open on January 11 unless they were given substantially increased purses.

Negotioations have finally been completed by horse owners and Nassau Racing Association. When the track will open rests with the Racing Commission. From left Mr. Ferguson, RHOA, Mr. David Strachan, Racing Secretary and Handicapper, Mr. George Capron, BRHOTF, and Mr. Colebrook, Racing Controller for NRA.

(3) Wellington Ferguson, Horse Owners Association president, says they can't stop racing.

(4) Racing pact goes to Wilson. Wellington Ferguson, BHDA, David Strachan, George Capron, and Arthur Colebrooke.

The Very Good Old Days at Hobby Horse Hall

Mr. Dencil Rolle owner of the winning horse "Idle Dice" is seen holding the winning trophy from L-R Mr. George McKinney, Mr. Franklyn Wilson. Racing commission chairman, former Prime Minister of the Bahamas Rt. Hon. Hubert A. Ingraham, Mrs. Arthur Colebrook, unidentified groom jockey Austin Saunders atop "Idle Dice" Asst. Trainer Whitey Stubbs, James "Fuzzy" Stubbs, trainer Mr. Rolle, Valentine Grimes, and Mr. Arthur Colebrook General Manager of Hobby Horse Hall.

Tuesday, January 11

Low returns on first day.

Deputy prime minister pressed the button to officially open the 1977 race season. Mr. Adrian D'Aguilar, the official starter, looks on.

Winner of the Philip Pinder Cup Race, Shaheen ridden by Herbert Cartwright poses with (1. to 4.) co-owner J. Henry Bostwick, trainer Lionel Wallace, Basil Huyler, Melissa Aranha, co-owner, and Philip Pinder sponsor of the race. Photo: Derek Smith.

Late surge earns Garth Fraser's Capricorn the Executive Printers Trophy.

Saturday, March 26
by Tyrone Olander
Bernie Is a Real Flag Carrier

"With the colors you have on, there was no doubt you would have won," said Prime Minister Lynden O. Pindling during the presentation ceremonies after the running of the prestigious Prime Minister Cup Race. (What a way to extol patriotism.)

Young jockey sensation Bernard Richardson won the race aboard Make Away, a four-year-old stallion owned by Prince Davis. Jockey Richardson was wearing a shirt in the national flag colors while winning the grueling nine-furlong race. Make Away was trained by Jim McKenzie.

Prior to the prime minister's congratulatory remarks, Racing Commission chairman Mr. Franklyn Wilson spoke and said in 1967 a lot of traditions were started, and the Prime Minister's Cup Race was among them. However, since the race started, it was opened to the top-class horses only.

Favorite island rule (6) during the fifth race suffered an apparent heart attack and threw the jockey Sidney Hamilton clear of injury. The 10 year old stallion owned by Vincent D. P. Roberts died on the track. However, island rule has sired several horses during his lifetime that are champions. Pictured is the horse writhing in pain, while jockey Hamilton watches. Photo: Wendell Cleare.

Prime Minister Cup Winners 1967 to 1977

1967	Old Libe
Owner:	Lawrence Lightbourn
Trainer:	David Strachan
Jockey:	C. Outten

1968	Yama
Owner:	Netlea Strachan
Trainer:	David Strachan
Jockey:	Austin Saunders

1969   Regal Ranger
Owner: Michael Darville
Trainer: Frank C. Walker
Jockey: Gary Bain

1970   Regal Ranger
Owner: Michael Darville
Trainer: Frank C. Walker
Jockey: George Godet

1971   Barbara
Owner: Wellington Hamilton
Trainer: Advis Hall
Jockey: Lionel Saunders

1972   Reina De Wyon
Owner: Cynthia Rolle
Trainer: Ellison Rolle
Jockey: John Bain

1973   Horan Shoran
Owner: Vivian Thompson
Trainer: Vivian Thompson
Jockey: S. McNeil

1974   Count Zorich
Owner: Victor Calridge
Trainer: Melvin Godet
Jockey: Austin Saunders

1975	Count Zorich
Owner:	Victor Claridge
Trainer:	Charles Moxey
Jockey:	Austin Saunders

1977

Derby Day Gift to Six Jockeys Racing fans will be surprised to see the returns of six top jockeys to the saddle again.

It's official that the six jockeys who have been suspended by the Racing Commission for three years following indifferent riding last season have been given the go-ahead to ride again, jockeys John Bain, Gary Bain, Anthony Saunders, Stan McNeil, Kevin Johnson, and Joe Horton.

Bain comes back a big winner.

John Bain returned to the saddle in magnificent style Friday when he booted home a season and career high of five winners. Of the six jockeys suspended at the end of last season, only John Bain and Joe Horton returned to the saddle on Friday.

Friday, April 1

KING OF THOROUGHBREDS — Jockey Glen Serchwell mounts in expression of victory Friday after bringing native bred Count Zorich from behind to capture a gruelling nine-furlong run which was designed especially for thoroughbred horses. Finishing a full length behind Count Zorich, is Stuttering Lou which carried jockey Prince Newbold and top weight of 140 pounds. Post Lady, ridden by returning jockey John Bain, did not run in the money as Winsome Charlie finished third under little R. Taylor.

King of Thoroughbreds jockey Glen Serchwell rides Count Zorich to victory over Stuttering Lou.

Gibbs pilots Philip Pinder's King Solomon to Bahamian Derby victory.

Philip Pinder issued a challenge to any horse to contest Count Zorich over nine furlongs for a $1,000 winner-take-all match race. Two hundred fifty-four years ago, John Pinder's Rodney was the king of Thoroughbreds on the racing circuit in the Bahamas (horse racing, a Pinder's Dynasty).

Count Zorich was no match for Keith Finley's Stuttering Lou in the $1,000 match race.

Saturday, April 2

DERBY WINNER – A well-conditioned King Solomon is pictured at the winner's circle following Saturday's close victory over Born To Win in the Second Bahamian Derby. Atop King Solomon is slick-riding Alfred Gibbs. The inset shows Gibbs whipping King Solomon across the finish line with Born To Win, ridden by Glen Serchwell, in hot pursuit. Standing second from right is former Miss Bahamas Sonia Chipman who presented the trophies to owner Philip Pinder (third from left) and trainer Melvin Godet (fourth from left). At far left is Bradley Roberts of Bahamas Blenders who helped to sponsor the $5,000 Derby. ––E. Bruce Delancey photos.

SPECIAL GUEST AT HHRT....... Mr. and Mrs. Thomas Fitzgerald, of New York was special guest of the Nassau Racing Association and Hobby Horse Hall Race Track on Saturday past. Mr. Fitzgerald is the president of New York Racing Association Incorporated, operators of the Aqueduct, Belmont and Saratoga circuits in New York. The three tracks are reputed to carry a handle of over 800 million dollars per year. The Fitzgeralds are house guest of Mr. and Mrs. Roberts J. Wilbur. Mr. Wilbur is a long time friend and vice president and General Manager of Morgan Guaranty Trust Company in Nassau. Pictured with the Fitzgerald (second and third from right) and Wilburs at the local race track on Saturday are right, Mr. George McKinney, President of N.R.A., Mr. Franklyn Wilson M.P. Chairman of the Racing Commission, centre, and Mr. Arthur Colebrook Jr. Managing Director of N.R.A. left.

Stuttering Lou proves too tough for Count

Philip Pinder's Count Zorich was "absolutely no match" for Stuttering Lou when the two highly-acclaimed thoroughbreds hooked up Saturday afternoon at the Hobby Horse Race Track.

There was no parimutuel betting on the nine furlong match race but a brief consensus of the hand betting showed the native bred Count Zorich the slight favourite.

When the gates opened, veteran rider Austin Saunders was quick to pushing Count Zorich to a leading position on the inside. But, Joe Sweeting Jr. had been all psyched up on how to ride Jethro Finley's Stuttering Lou and he kept pace and took full command after the first turn. Stuttering Lou galloped the final five furlongs completely unchallenged and the five length spread at the finish was ample proof of what kind of match the race was.

Both Count Zorich and Stuttering Lou carried equal weight of 120 pounds. On April Fool's Day, Glen Serebwell was a triumphant jockey aboard Count Zorich when they covered the nine furlong journey in a 1:59.5 seconds for a handicap win over Stuttering Lou which carried top weight of 140 pounds including jockey Prince Newbold.

NO MATCH — Jockey Joe Sweeting Jr. hurls his whip high in the air as he and Jethro Finley's Stuttering Lou cruise to an easy five-length victory over Philip Pinder's native bred Count Zorich which was ridden by leading jockey Austin Saunders. The match race victory boosted Finley's claim that Stuttering Lou is the top horse now racing at Hobby Horse Race Track.

Signing of challenge match.

Pictured in the office of managing Director, Mr. Arthur Colebrook, Mr. J. J. Finley (right) and Mr. Hilton sign as agreement for their challenge match for a nine-furlong race, winner-take-all $5,000.00 purse, between Maestro a three-year-old thoroughbred owned by Mr. Hilton running in Florida and Mr. Finley's Stuttering Lou a three-year-old-gelding reputed on local track.

Friday April 15
Racing Ends at HHRT

Hobby Horse Racetrack closed the 1977 race season, and from all indications, this is the final race season at the present location.

Special guest at the racetrack, deputy prime minister and minister of finance, Mr. A. D. Hanna, in his address to the racing fans, said that this is to be the last year for racing at this site, and he also said that should there be horse racing next year it would definitely be at a new site.

TRAINER OF THE YEAR, Mr. Henry Burrows and Jockey-of-the-Year, Austin Saunders, presented Mr. Franklyn Wilson, the Racing Commission chairman, with a plaque in appreciation of his services on behalf of the jockeys, trainers grooms and horse-owners. The plaque which reads: "In appreciation for his untiring effort towards upgrading horse racing in the Bahamas and in recognition of his great concern for the small man in horse racing." Pictured along with Mr. Wilson, Mr. Burrows, and jockey Saunders is the Deputy Prime Minister, Mr. Arthur Hanna, special guest of Nassau Racing Association. *(Photo: TYRONE O'LANDER.)*

Trainer of the Year, the late Henry Burrows, and Jockey of the Year, Austin Saunders, presented Mr. Franklyn Wilson, the Racing Commission chairman, with a plaque in appreciation of his services on behalf of the jockeys, trainers, grooms, and horse owners. The plaque reads "In appreciation for his untiring effort toward ungrading horse racing in the Bahamas, and in recognition of his great concern for the small man in horse racing."

Keith Finley's Stuttering Lou, Horse of the Year, trained by Tommy Demeritte and ridden by Anthony Saunders.

Young oncoming jockey sensation Barry Arthur also received a trophy from the deputy prime minister.

Sun Tiger won the Slowest Horse race, ridden by Austin Saunders––$100 winner take all.

The annual running of the Racing Commission Two-Year-Old Cup Race was cancelled!

A problem arose when top Executive, a Thoroughbred owned by Alphonso "Boogaloo" Elliott, entered the Two-Year-Old Race. Several trainers voiced their disagreement over the eligibility of the horse, which was designed specifically for native-bred horses only.

(1) July 19, 1977, the PLP won the general election.
(2) August 30, 1977, Bay Street parade on future of horse racing.

BAHAMAS Race Horse Owners Association president, Wellington Ferguson (right) is shown heading the demonstrators today at the start of the three-day protest for an official statement on horse racing from government.

John Chipman, owner of seven horses at the race track makes his point clear while relating his feelings today over government silence of the immediate future of horse racing. Pictures: Jeffrey Thompson.

(3) Nine placard-wearing horsemen from the Bahamas Racehorse Owners and Trainers Federation began their joint three-day picketing today on Bay Street. The men paraded between East and Parliament Streets, calling on government to make an official statement on horse racing for 1978. Spontaneous gathering of curious spectators and tourists watched from the sidewalks as the placard-bearing demonstrators paraded outside the House of Assembly.

Mr. John Chipman, who owns seven horses, said this demonstration should have started before the election, and everything would have been fine. The people should have moved the protest a long time ago. Mr. Chipman also said that if there is no racing next season, the Racing Commission should give the horse owners money from the benevolent fund so that they can keep their animals until there is racing. The money, they say, can be allocated from the benevolent fund to be used by horse owners in emergency situations and for hardships (the Racing Commission has control of the fund).

Bay Street parade on future of racing

AUG 31 1977

Angry horsemen
demand answer

Price: 25c (Out Islands: 30c)

SEP 6 1977

R SE
CING
THE
NLY
ZED GAMBLING
BAHAMIANS

PLEASE
MR HANNA
WE HELPED
YOU.
HELP US!

Horse protest
in fifth day

TWO of the demonstrators
representing the BRHOA and
the RHOTF are shown
picketing yesterday outside
the House of Assembly, Bay
Street. [Photo: DEREK
SMITH].

Some of the placards worn by the protesters read "Unfair Racing
Commission do not care," "No racing, no jobs!" "Is it really better
in the Bahamas for Bahamians and racehorses?" and "Please, Mr.
Hanna, we need you. Help us!"

344

September 7, 1977
Roadworks Continue at Hobby Horse Track

Hobby Horse Hall Race Track Demolished

Ministry of Works employees are shown today operating a bulldozer and other vehicles during construction on a dual roadway running through the back stretch of the Hobby Horse Race Track.

THE BACK-STRETCH AT THE RACE TRACK? - That's right. This is what it looks like today as government begin laying down a new dual highway in the Cable Beach area to serve the hotel area better and in preparation for government's huge Cable Beach convention/casino complex to be built there. The Tribune understands government will now stop the road-building and repair this back-straight so that racing can be held for one more season at Hobby Horse Race Track.

Horsemen proposed that government utilize $24,000 from the benevolent fund to repair track so that there can be racing for one more year at Hobby Horse Hall.

Representatives from Ladbroke, Britain's largest gambling conglomerate, were recently in Nassau for talks with government on horse racing.

Racing Commission's chairman, Mr. Franklyn Wilson, confirmed that discussions were going on with Ladbroke and others and stated, at the time, he "confidently expects a new racetrack to be built."

Talks broke down with Ladbroke!

Horse protest in fifth day.

Starved racehorse drops dead.

Floridians fly feed to starving animals!

Horses shipped
OCT 31 1977
over to Miami

THREE thoroughbred horses were shipped to Miami yesterday where they will be trained for racing at Florida tracks early next year.

Casino Gold, owned by Police Supt. Cyril Joseph, Post Lady, owned by Churtum Munroe, and Star of Gemini, owned by politician Philip Pinder, were loaded aboard the mv Marcella H yesterday afternoon.

After reaching Miami, the horses were taken into quarantine and will be held for over a week. Following their isolation period, the thoroughbreds will be examined by Florida authorities.

Once the animals are declared fit, they will be transferred to the Calder Race Track in Hialeah where they will be trained by Bahamian Carl Armbrister.

The horses, which were imported from the US as yearlings and had each won four racing medals, will race at various Florida tracks after they are pronounced fit by Mr. Armbrister.

Contacted today, Mr. Philip Pinder said he planned to keep his Star of Gemini in Florida "indefinitely."

"It won't make sense to bring them back without a racing track here," he told The Tribune.

Mr. Pinder owns four other horses at Hobby Horse Race Track. "They eat well and they've got good care," he said. "I don't have any plans for selling them. Race horses are not docile. The chance of selling them are zero. I'll just have to see what happens," he said.

Doubts over the future of horse racing in the Bahamas rose after government's takeover of the track at the end of last season to build a giant convention and casino complex at the site.

Government has yet to issue a statement concerning the future of horse racing. Meanwhile, construction on a dual carriageway over part of the race track has begun.

The horse racing problem is now of international interest. Stories on Hobby Hall have been carried in American and Canadian newspapers.

On Saturday, north Miami Beach horse owner Bonni Denmark, accompanied by Sherry Schlueter, a Broward County Humane Society inspector, arrived in Nassau with two tons of food and hay for starving horses at the track.

An article in the Miami Herald on the "starving" horses and "rat infested stables" prompted Mrs. Denmark to collect donations for the feed and set up an emergency relief.

The two Florida women flew back yesterday, but are expected to return here following a meeting the Bahamas Racing Commission will hold tomorrow evening.

Americans to Take Abandoned Horses

Mrs. Donni Denmark and Mrs. Sherry Schlueter, from the Broward County Humane Society in Miami, Florida, organized emergency relief feed for the animals. Mr. Levarity Deveaux, secretary of BRHOA, Mr. Wellington Ferguson, and the late Henry Burrows requested their help.

November 26, 1977
Ten More Horses Flown Out

VOL. LXXIV. No. 283   Saturday, October 29, 1977   Price: 25c (Out Islands: 30c)

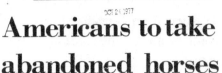

Americans to take abandoned horses

VOL. LXXIV. No. 283   Saturday, October 29, 1977

Floridians fly feed to starving animals

Americans to Take Abandoned Horses

A North Miami Beach horse owner was so moved by a *Miami Herald* story about racehorses being left to starve in the Bahamas that she organized a relief mission through friends.

The result of Mrs. Donni Denmark's efforts were seen yesterday when the first of three planeloads of feed and hay were flown from Fort Lauderdale to Nassau by Mackey Airlines free of charge. The last planeload--two tons of feed and hay in all--arrived this morning for the 140 horses that have been abandoned at the Hobby Horse Racetrack stables.

The emergency supplies are being stored at the Bahamas Humane Society, and ways were being worked out today as to how best to distribute the feed to the starving animals.

Ten horses have reportedly died at the track of malnutrition or starvation since government's silence on repeated horse owners' requests as to whether there would be any racing come January when the racing season normally opens.

Following a meeting this morning between officers of the Bahamian Horse Owners Association and the Florida and Bahamian Humane Society officials, it has been decided that several abandoned animals will be allowed to be taken and cared for by Florida interests.

At this morning's meeting were Mr. George Capron, president of the Bahamas Horse Owners and Trainers Federation: Henry Burrows, owner of Paradise Island Racing Stables; Wellington Ferguson, president of the Bahamas Racehorse Owners Association; Mrs. Sherry Schlueter, an investigating officer with the Broward County Humane Society in Florida; and Mrs. Denmark.

"It was a very beneficial meeting. We saw the condition of the horses at the track, and the owners seem most concerned for their animals. They will let us take the animals," said Mrs. Denmark.

Mrs. Denmark flew in to Nassau yesterday with the first supplies accompanied by Mrs. Schlueter.

Mr. Levarity Deveaux, general secretary of the Bahamas Racehorse Owners Association, shown at Hobby Horse Racetrack stables this morning, examining the state of the horses.

"I became concerned as a horse lover when I first read about the plight of the animals over here in an article in Tuesday's *Miami Herald*," Mrs. Denmark told the *Tribune* today. The article headlined "Horses Left to Starve in the Bahamas," accompanied by a colored picture of a starving horse at the track, was run on the front page of the *Herald* this week.

Mrs. Denmark said she called some of her friends, who made donations to her, and she managed to get a good break from her feed store to buy a ton of hay and feed.

She gave Colonel Mackey, the head of Mackey Airlines, a call. She had never even met him, but he agreed to fly the food in for the horses free of charge. "He's a very generous man," said Mrs. Denmark.

Since she and Mrs. Schlueter have been here, both are "most impressed" with the Bahamas Humane Society. "I've never met such dedication, enthusiasm, and compassion," said Mrs. Denmark. "I can't say enough for them."

George Capron brought the plight of the local horses to the attention of the world press, which was covering the Queen's tour here last week.

United Press International, the *Miami Herald* and Miami News, Channel 7 in Chicago, and a Canadian newspaper have picked up the story.

And yesterday, the Bahamas Tourism Office in Chicago was picketed for a while over the "starving horses" report.

Yesterday, meetings were held with Claude Smith, director of agriculture, Trent, the two Florida women, and Cyril Stevenson, head of Bahamas Information Services.

Notices were prepared and read over the national radio station, saying that the Bahamas Humane Society was anxious to talk to any racehorse owner who wanted to find a good home for his horse in the USA.

Interested persons were asked to call the Humane Society, where a twenty-four-hour service was being maintained over this weekend.

"We want to do whatever is humanly possible to alleviate the suffering of these poor animals," a Humane Society spokesman said. Therefore, someone will be on duty all day and all night at the Humane Society.

Already today the Humane Society has had calls from horse lovers throughout the USA, from Ohio, Michigan, Chicago, and Florida, from people who are willing to give these horses a home.

Horse owners who wish to give up their horses will not be paid, said Mrs. Denmark, since all that is being offered is to find the animals nice homes with horse lovers.

However, carriage of the animals back to Florida will cost a lot of money, besides finding the necessary $70 per animal for the week's quarantine, which is obligatory under U.S. regulations.

A fund is being opened in Florida through the Broward County Humane Society for animal lovers to send donations to help the Bahamian Horses Relief, said Mrs. Schlueter.

It is expected that final details regarding the carriage of the horses out of the country will be worked out following a meeting.

Two Florida women pictured with Bahamas racehorse owners at the Bahamas Humane Society today with one of the starving horses. Mrs. Donni Denmark (*at right*) organized emergency relief food supplies for the animals in Florida with the help of Mrs. Sherry Schlueter from the Broward County Humane Society in Florida (*second right*). *Standing from left*: Wellington Ferguson, president of the Horse Owners Association; Levarity Deveaux, general secretary to the association; Henry Burrows, vice president; and George Capron, president of the Horse Owners and Trainers Federation. (Photo: Oswald Hanna.)

Nassau and Bahama Islands Reading

Saturday, November 26, 1977

Ten More Starved Horses Flown Out
By Athena Damianos

Ten gaunt, sore infested race horses were flown to Florida by animal carrier today for adoption. But they had a long wait at the airport from 8:30 this morning until the plane arrived around noontime.

The animals were put into quarantine immediately after they arrived in Florida. If they are declared fit by U.S. health officials after a one week period, the horses will be trucked to Palm Springs, where they will await adoption.

Travelling with the skinny horses was a healthy three-year-old thoroughbred owned by Israel Hall.

According to a relative, the horse was sent to Florida for racing. "There's no guarantee to say whether he'll stay indefinitely," the relative said. "He's going away simply because there's no racing happening here."

Today's shipment marked the second wave of horses to be transported to Florida by Mrs. Sherry Schlueter, an investigating officer from the Broward County, Florida, Humane Society, and Mrs. Bonnie Denmark, a north Miami Beach rancher.

Volunteer help today described the horses as being "in very bad condition."

Seven of the animals have been under the care of the Bahamas Humane Society for the past month. But although

Two humane society members taking it upon themselves to make the long wait for the air transport plane a little easier for the animals by providing the horses with some water. *(Photo: Oswald Hanna.)* they have received good care, their bodies are covered with sores and their bones protrude like sticks. Many of the animals are suffering from hoof rot.

"It will take from six months to a year to get these horses back in good shape again," a local horse owner commented. "If you suddenly stuff them they'll get choleric. Many of them are prone to choleric now."

The horses were rescued from the rat infested Hobby Hall Race Track. It is understood that over 100 starving horses have been left abandoned at the track by owners who are not prepared to spend money for feed if there is to be no racing here this coming season.

The move to give the horses for adoption came after government refused to say whether the 1978 racing season would open. Many horse owners now find themselves stuck with non-profit animals they claim they cannot afford to keep.

Just over a week ago, the first wave of fourteen rescued horses were trucked to Mrs. Bonnie Denmark's north Palm Springs stable after undergoing a seven day quarantine period. Mrs. Denmark heard of the plight of the Nassau horses in the Miami Herald and launched an emergency rescue measure through friends to get food for them. Two tons of feed was flown in for the animals from Florida.

Most of the horses were sold at a non-profit $311. The cost covers transportation, quarantine and food.

Although $311 is "a little high" for an animal without registration papers, The Tribune was told that the new owners were "happy" with the deal.

"It is not known whether any more horses will be shipped to Florida for adoption," Humane Society Inspector Neil Trent said recently.

Ten gaunt, sore infested race horses were flown to Florida by animal carrier today. Today's shipment marked the second wave of race horses to be transported to Florida by Mrs. Sherry Schlueter.

The move to give the horses up for adoption came after The Bahamas Racing Commission refused to say whether the 1978 racing season would be opened. Many horse owners now find themselves stuck with non-profit animals they claim they cannot afford to keep!

No More Racing

It's official. The Hobby Horse Hall Racetrack is closed for good.

Will the Bahamian Racing fans enjoy Ms. Lene's most tasty turkey drumsticks after a day of racing again? Or the sound of the bugle indicating the horses are entering the track or racetrack chants like "Ride him, Gary," "Hold the man horse, just like that," "If you beat him, I will eat him," "Scorch him now," "Catch that," or the voice of track announcer Sidney French, "Shoo-Bill for the lead," and musical renditions of "Fools rush in," "You don't know what you got until you lose it," and characters like Mingio (Albert Woods) dancing Paul Meeres's version of the Babaloo after Jack Daniel won a race, and "W. A. Weeks's Boo Boo bites his way to the finish line!" again? Maybe!

The remains of Hobby Horse Hall as it exists today. Placing Judge Tower, stairway to the Stewards Tower, clubhouse (front view), and clubhouse (interior).

One of the oldest and most historical racecourses in the Western world closed after 182 years!

The only racetrack of its kind in the world.

The most significant tourist attraction the Bahamas ever had, Hobby Horse Hall.

The name that rolled on the tongue and brought a cheerful picture to the mind!

Thank You

Hobby Horse Hall Racetrack did not close for the lack of attendance or the enthusiasm of the racing fans but for the development of the Cable Beach Hotel and Casino Complex, and there is no planning for another racetrack for the future.

Noted Bahamian Horse owners and the name of their Race Horses from 1844-1977

Governor Benvenutto Mathews (Lapidog)

John Pinder (Rodney)
Cory Damiands (Sansovin)
A. H. Sands (Lord Conroy)
Lady Eitienne Dupuch (Brooks Carlisle)
A.F. Adderley (Kismet)
Alva Brook "THE SHEIK"
W.A. WEEKES (Semibrave High Ball)
R.R. Farrington (Day Break)
Mrs R.T. Symonette (Mischief)
Mr Charles F Bethel (Brave Mark)
H.G. Christies ("Cape Town" "Sun Charmer")
Allan Roberts (Arab)
Mr Stanley Adderley "Dollie"
R. W. Farrington "Banco"
T.B. Thompson "Blucher"
John McCarthy "Capt. Desmond"
Mr Brown "Ida"
C. A. Fox "Jim"
The Pyfrom brothers "Champions"
Lady Eunice Oaks "Sea Biscuit"
"Sir Harry" ANZAC "Smokey"
G.C. Cash "Dimple" - "Ace"
N.J. French "Coronation Biller Weel"
Paul Meeres Bamm Sookey
Lennis Lightbourne "War Admiral"
Sir Oswald A. Bancroft "Muse"
Mrs. Moore "Play Boy" - "Rani"

Charles Wolfe - "Black Lady"
Philip Pinder - "Canada Dry" - "King Solomon"
A. B. Malcolm - "Kanaka"
ASA Pritchard - "Eclipse"
Geroge Murphy - "Chance"
Brice Pinder - "Jane Mac"
Dr. K.V.A. Rogers "Branwen"
Robert W. Turnquest "Ram Su"
Corinne Mitchell "Kia Mesha"
Sigfried Amoury "Gaucho"
H. N. Chipman "King"
Sir Victor Sassoon "Nassau Eve" - "Misty Eve"
Hon. O. H. Curry "Tricks"
Lawerence Lightbourn "Old Libe"
Felix Johnson "Ruth Blood"
G.F. Dillet - "Shirley Gray"
Harold Smith - "Mutt"
B. K. Thompson "Dirty Dicks"
Nico Maillis "Haille Selassie"
Fred Smith "Wildfire"
Maury Roberts "Omaha"
Mr. Rudolph Young "Mussolini"
Fread McKay "Steve Wall"
John Bastian - "Game Choser"
Basil Huyler Sr "Steplight"
Mr Bert Cambrige "Good News"
Mr Joseph Joe Billy Rolle - Grey Stone "Emily"
Charles Williams "No-GO"
Charles Moss "Papa Doperlas"
Mr. Otram Rahming Capt Kidd
A.F. Pindling "Gravel Gertis"
K.M. Thompson "Asavache" - "Borasco"
V.P. Munnings - Mercy Percy" - "Hot Love"
Leroy Miller - "City Pride"
Charles Pinder Jubilee
L.N. Wells "Gallant Lady" - "Go Go Girl"

Wellington Ferguson "Mr Brite" - "Mama Brite"
Albert Lloyd "Thunder" "Mystery"
Alphonso Elliott "Top Executive" - "Pac Buster"
Kenneth Seymour "Air Queen" - "Air Dance"
Victor Claridge "Count Zorich"
Garth Fraser "Capricorn" - "RU Happy"
Gary Wallace "Neysas Joy"
Audley Archer "Lady Archbold" - "Bold Child"
L.C. Brice "Shoo Fly" - "Beauty"
Gurth Gonzalez "Conch Salad" - "Speedy Gonzalez"
Sidney French "Jungle Queen" - "Vonwise"
George Capron "Gone Away" - "Bundio"
Reginald Pratt "Queen of Hearts"
Jetrho Finlry "Stultering Lu"
Alice Musgrove "Katunga"
Louis Grammatico "Coast Guard" - "Italian Rose"
Theophilis Fritz "Alteza" - "Gale of Wind"
Wenzel Gilten "Git O Git"
Nelson Chipman "Dat Like Dat"
Melvin Godet "Fly Away" - "Patches"
Eric Cooper "Winged Duchess" - "Poetry Inmotion"
William Curtis "Mar Cheri"
J Henry Bostwick "Markell"
P.C. Forsythe "Mark Twain"
Kennth Francis "Soul Dancer"
Bruce Deveaux "Echo"
Ronald Renegade Kemp "Torino" - "The Kid"
Dr John Godet "Pams ACE" "El - Spiro"
Levarity Deveaux "Shasada"
L.T. Hilton "Baggers Delight" - "Senilossa"
John Tilliacos "Venus"
Frank Walker "Friendship Child" "Nadds Child"
Ezekial Black "Go Sugar"
Vivian Thompson "Swamp Fire"
Kingsley Wilson "Vanguard" - "Four Roses"
Peter Mackey "Mackey Dog"

Wilfred Knowles "Winsome Charles
Vincent DePaul Roberts "Bon Bah Rose" - "Appian Way"
Erwin Knowles "Bambino"
Paul Norton "Clipper"
David Strachan "Yama"
Hugh Strachan "Fisherman" "Oh My"
Nigel Ingraham "Spanish Rose"
Gene Chea "Yellow Elder"
Sam "Bulla" Bowe Brave Boy "Fun"
A.D. Hanna "Brave Boy" "Fun"
E.V. Walker E.V's Child
James Lamm "Mandingo"
Prince Davis "Make a Way"
Alfred Brown "Magic Prince"
Rowena Sweeting "Sir Native"
Tome Ferguson "Miss H.T."
Rick Penn "Von Herb" - "Regal Star"
Basil Butler "Big Smer"
Mr Todd "Queen of Colmell" - "Chiccarney" - "Wendy B"
John Darville "Miss Omolene" "Miss Purina"
Moira Kennedy "Esrelita"
Enid Lewis "Dedi" - "Debi"
E. H. Godet "Blue Skies" "Dan Patch"
Jim McKenzie "Concha Bay"
Noel Bastian "Respect Toy"
Claude Knowles "County"
Neville Smith "Golden Missile"
Harcourt Bastian "Black Gold" - "Popeye"
Mario Parotti "Red Eagle" "Mrs Pumpkin"
H Smith "Mrs Millie"
Cecil Wallace-Whitfield "Cochise"
L M Bowe "Tony"
John Chipman "Run Joe" - "Aquarius"
Glen Holmes "Reina De Whoyon"

Thad Johnson "Glamour Gal" - "Princess Montaqu"
Junior Key "Crow Dancer"
Henry Burrows "Mr B"
Charlie Ageeb "Royal Crown"
Hickley Heastie "Encino"

Author's Note

In 1977, it was a rainy race day at Hobby Horse Hall, and the long shots were the norm of the day. I was a patrol judge at the two-furlong pole. After the race, I decided to walk back to the pavilion. By the time I reached the clubhouse, it was cleared.

I decided to go to the shack on the infield to get some water, something I have never done before. To my surprise, canisters of racing films were discarded all over the room. A positive thought came to me, and I selected six canisters of racing films, which I horded for twenty-three years. After spending three years in the Dominican Republic as president and managing director of Tropical Hotel and Casino Management Company, I decided it was high time for me to have those films edited and to have nostalgia nights of racing from Hobby Horse Hall Racetrack at the Southerners Lounge and Mr. T's Sporting Lounge for the old horse racing fans. After the editing of the films, being air-bound, another positive thought embellished my mind that there was more to horse racing from Hobby Horse Hall. Why don't you do a documentary on horse racing in the Bahamas? The rest is history. To this day, those edited films for the nostalgia racing from Hobby Horse Hall race fans have never been shown publicly.

In 1977, Hobby Horse Hall Racetrack closed. Mr. Oscar Johnson and Mr. Franklyn Wilson lost grace in the PLP. The PLP won the 1977 election, and Mr. Preston Albury was appointed Racing Commission chairman. The Paradise Island bridge was fully regaled with balloons and posters welcoming Mr. George Myers as their senior VP managing director. Mr. Peter Streit, CEO of Jack Tar Hotel Management Co. of

Dallas, Texas, won the bid to manage all the Bahamas government hotels: Ambassador Beach Hotel and Emerald Beach Hotel and the Balmoral Beach Hotel.

Mr. Victor Lownes, CEO of Playboy Casinos, London, was granted a casino gaming license to operate a casino in the Ambassador Beach Hotel on Cable Beach (Playboy Casino) in 1978.

In 1978, Mr. Preston Albury was appointed chairman of the Select Committee on Horse and Dog Racing in the Bahamas. Phillip Smith, Garnet J. Levarity, and C. Leander Minnis were made committee members. It is interesting to note that it was alleged that the PLP government was all set to own all the casinos in the Bahamas and to have the existing casino operators in Nassau and Freeport manage the casino. At the fair management fee, the PLP government realized that they could not continue to keep Bahamians from a play of game of chance in the casinos, and the only way to do it was to own it so the Bahamian dollar could stay home.

The late Mr. Everette Bannister Office was in place on property owned by Jack Davis and James Crosby. Top executive of Resorts International became livid on hearing of the government's future plans. The Right Honorable Prime Minister Sir Lynden O. Pindling made a 360-degree turn, and it never happened. Only one person alive can tell us why the government did not continue with the plan, and that is the former governor-general of the Bahamas, Mr. A. D. Hanna. When a question is asked about the subject matter, Mr. Hanna will say the Right Honorable Sir Lynden O. Pindling was a pragmatic fellow!

Author's Note

Report of Select Committee on Horse and Dog Racing in the Bahamas

Mr. Speaker:

The Select Committee appointed by you on June 21, 1978, to take into consideration the question of horse and dog racing in the Bahamas and all matters relating thereto and connected therewith, with power to send for persons and papers and with leave to sit during the recess beg leave to report as follows:

Your committee found that horse racing in the Bahamas continued for a long time up to the year 1977 when it was discontinued as the land upon which the racetrack was erected was required by the Hotel Corporation of the Bahamas for extensive tourist-oriented development. The committee also found that the government, in anticipation of the above move, for some years now, has made available one hundred acres of land at Gladstone Road in New Providence for the future development of horse racing.

Email address: heresataxi@yahoo.com
Telephone numbers: (242) 327-8331; (242) 451-3594

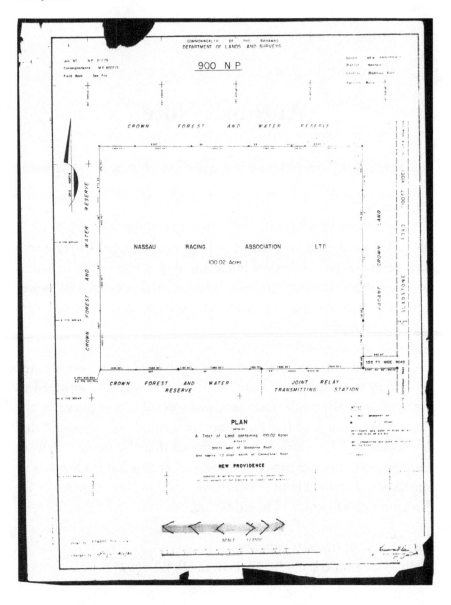

The committee also learned that the government preferred that the development of a racetrack should be carried out by persons other than the government.

So far as dog racing is concerned, the committee was informed that although the government was prepared to allow dog racing in

Freeport, it was felt that the population in Freeport was insufficient to support a properly operated dog racecourse.

The committee considered the whole question, referred to it at length, and has come to the conclusion and recommends that the government continues its efforts to encourage the development of a racetrack for horses in New Providence and was informed that the Gladstone Road site was the most adequate and desirable location.

It was suggested to the committee that dog racing be allowed to be operated in conjunction with and on the same premises as the horse track at such times and for such periods of the year as the government may consider desirable, and in this regard, it was suggested to the committee that the horse racing season be extended to six months and dog racing for perhaps a little longer.

Your committee now recommends the following:

i.   That horse racing should commence the first Saturday in January, which will consist of forty race meets. The last race to be held on Easter Monday.

ii.   With regard to dog racing, your committee recommends that it should commence the last Saturday night in May and continue for forty meets, the same as horse racing.

iii. Your committee also recommends there should only be two (2) race meets per week for horses and dogs on Tuesdays and Saturdays. The dog racing is to be held after horse racing subject to approval.

Dated this nineteenth day of October 1978.

Author's Note

Preston H. Albury (Chairman)
Philip P. Smith
Garnet J. Levarity
C. Leander Minnis

After realizing that the Bahamas government was 100 percent in support of horse racing and dog racing, a Bahamian group was formed under the trading name Nassau Race Co. In principle, the Bahamas government gave them a lease of crown land 100.2 acres in the Gladstone Road area for fifty years. Coming on stream at the same time was a commercial bank under the trading name Wellington Bank. NRC funds were deposited in the said bank, and in principle, application for a business venture loan was approved. One or two of the board members of NRC heard some negative reports about the bank's solvency and registered to have their share reimbursed to them. The rest of the directors did not take heed, and the bank ran away with their deposits. The NRC directors wanted the government to bail them out because government failed to have the said bank post a bond for security reasons. Government saw it differently and stated that they would have some form of conflict of interest but would give all the infrastructure to support horse racing, e.g., road, water, electricity, land, and telephone, but we would not build a racetrack.

A bad stigma developed every time a noted foreign company that operated racetracks around the world made an offer to build a racetrack. It was alleged that the local group want 10 percent up front to recoup their losses. Local interests in the horse racing had declined for a long time.

In 1999–2000 the FMN government realized that funds still existed in the Racing Commission bank accounts, and they wanted to disburse the funds to those that were entitled to it. I was asked to be on the committee for that purpose. I told them, based on my research, all monies derived from horse racing in the Bahamas could only be disbursed by a bona fide racing commission of the Bahamas, not by a selected group as stated in the Racing Commission Act chapter 386 of Statue Laws of the Bahamas. The FNM government sought consultants from the Attorney General Office on the matter, and they advised that chapter 386 of the Racing Commission Act of the Bahamas has to be enforced enacted!

In 2001, when the documentary on horse racing in the Bahamas was finished, a local group of reputable Bahamians was formed in principle, and they made an application to the then FNM government for the reintroduction of horse racing in the Bahamas, hoping that the FNM government would agree in principle, subject to some form of stipulations, but the request to reintroduce horse racing was denied.

In 2002, the PLP won the general election in 2003. With recommendation by the prime minister, Perry Gladstone Christie, to the governor-general, I was appointed chairman of the Bahamas Racing Commission for three years. I was very happy and hopeful for the return of horse racing in the Commonwealth, but to my dismay, I was Racing Commission chairman for six years without a mandate. The office of the Racing Commission never opened!

Author's Note

From 2003 to 2006, the rhetoric among the ministers of government was that the Bahamas Christian Council was against horse racing in the Bahamas. In 2006, at Transfiguration Baptist Church on Vesey and Market Street, where Mr. Lavoin "Bowe" Stuart was being funeralized, I was engaged in a dialogue with two senior ministers of the PLP government, and to my surprise, I was told to take a look at opening a racetrack in Freeport! I was astonished to believe what they were saying. It sounded like the Bahamas Christian Council has agreed for horse racing in Freeport but not New Providence (Nassau, it was food for thought). I immediately embarked on my own feasibility study of the Bahamas Christian Council members on an individual basis to get their true opinions on gaming in the Bahamas for Bahamians. I applied a psychological approach to the following members: Bishop Samuel Green, Bishop Simeon Hall, Bishop Albert Hepburn, Bishop T. G. Morrison, Reverend Dr. Charles Saunders, Bishop Neil Ellis, Dr. C. B. Moss, and Reverend Baltron Bethell. I made a phone call to each member and informed him that I, Ivan Abidial James, have a documentary on horse racing in the Bahamas, over two hundred years of lost rich Bahamian history. In response, they wanted to know when I could bring the documents to their representative church offices. In six weeks, I had the opportunity to meet with all the clergymen listed, with a minimum of one and a half hours' dialogue to discuss the documentary. Each clergyman was ecstatic to know that horse racing was indigenous in the lives of the citizens of the Bahamas. One minister stated that it is the only subculture of the Bahamas that white and black citizens endured together. They all agreed on the principle that they are there to win souls for Christ, not to be advocates for any form of gaming, and the incumbent government PLP or FMN should do the things they think is best for the people that give them the mandate to govern. Another comment was that the Right Honorable Sir Lynden O. Pindling in the early '70s saw the need for casino gaming in the colony for the tourist. The Christian Council opposed the idea collectively. The prime minister wrote to the Christian Council of his plans to implement casino gaming for the tourist, and the Bahamian dollar will not be the official currency to conduct business in the casino, and no one with gainful employment will be able to play a game of chance. The Christian Council still voiced their objection, but they saw the good benefits for the economic stability of the Bahamas. It is interesting to note that the Christian Council did not reply! Another comment was that in the election in 2007, none of the political parties should put on their platform lottery and the return of horse racing. Whoever won the election mandated by the people, they should go and legislate what was best for people of the Bahamas. No referendum!

The Christian Council would never openly campaign against the government that was mandated by the people to govern. What is so ironic is that I tried to get this message to the powers that be: the Right Honorable Hubert A. Ingraham, leader of the opposition (FNM) and the incumbent the Right Honorable Prime Minister Perry Gladstone Christie, but to no avail. They had no time available to see me, and the rest is history. The PLP lost and the FNM won the 2007 election.

Author's Note

In the first three years of the FNM governance, a lottery paper was compiled based on a feasibility study for a national lottery. In 2011, the FNM government dropped the lottery issue completely, and the Right Honorable Hubert A. Ingraham, prime minister of the Bahamas, never gave a reason for not presenting a lottery bill to parliament. In 2012 general election, the FNM lost. The PLP became the government, and immediately after the first one hundred days, a referendum date was set by the Right Honorable Perry Gladstone Christie for 2012 and was cancelled, and a new date was set for 2013. It is also interesting to note, in my political science theory, if an incumbent government wants something for the good of its people, they don't need a referendum; they would table a bill and pass it, then it would be gazetted, and it becomes law. If they are not in favor of the bill, then the government of the day will have a referendum for the people to decide.

The lottery referendum was held, and the people of the Bahamas voted a resounding *no*!

It is also interesting to note that the bolita bosses contracted the wrong messengers to convey the right message to the voters of the Bahamas. Out of the gate, they became confrontational with the clergy, and the rest is history!

In summary, horse racing was an integral part in the lives of the citizens of the Bahamas for over two hundred years and was definitely the first recorded national sport of the Bahamas and subculture of the Bahamian people. Hobby Horse Hall Racetrack is the first sporting seat that is recorded in our rich Bahamian history!

Horse racing was noted to be the sport of kings in the year 1711. The prestigious royal Ascot Racecourse was built in Windsor, England, during the reign of Queen Anne of England.

In the Bahamas, from 1790 to 1792, Hobby Horse Hall Racecourse was built simultaneously with the historic Fort Charlotte under the directive of the royal governor, the Earl of Dunmore, with his autocratic style of governance. Three hundred years later in England, to date, there are over fifty-seven racecourses, and the Bahamas has none! But it is fair to say that the Bahamas Hobby Horse Hall is the first documented one-mile oval racecourse in the Western world!

The Bahamas played a part in the horse racing industry of billions of dollars, but no more!

The horse racing industry exists in 80 percent of all the countries of the world, even in Muslim countries like Saudi Arabia, Kuwait, and Dubai, to name a few.

Thanks for being a part of this journey, a segment of over two hundred years of lost rich Bahamian history.

Finally, the million-dollar question to the Bahamian people, why don't we have horse racing--an industry that can sustain itself, a major tourist attraction?

Thank you,

Ivan "Abaco" James

The only cultural event that brought the white and black Bahamians together indigenously! Horse racing at Hobby Horse Hall.

Ivan Abidiel James
(242) 327 8331
heresataxi@yahoo.com

Book Review

Ivan, after reading your documentary manuscript on a segment of Bahamian history, I was inspired to fulfill my college dreams to write a segment of American history. Well done, Ivan!

Robert Ludlum
1927–2001

The Bahamas has a population of over three hundred thousand people, and only you, Ivan, had the vision to research a segment of lost rich Bahamian history, which is fascinating!

L. B. Johnson
Former ambassador to Washington
3 November 2001

This work by Ivan James, an industrious native of Market Street in Over-the-Hill, Nassau, should be read by every citizen and especially by schoolchildren in order that they might know.

Sir Orville A. Turnquest
Governor-general
2 July 2001

I was truly delighted when Ivan James came into my office several years ago and gave me an opportunity to read his wonderful work on horse racing in the Bahamas. It brought back a flood of memories.

Somewhere among my old photographs I have a picture of me, as a little girl, with my grandmother at Hobby Horse Hall. It was a day I have often remembered.

My family was much involved with horses. My grandfather, Jerome Eugene Pyfrom, kept five horses in stables in the backyard of his home on Augusta Street. My favorite was a molasses-colored mare named Jubilee. My father, Ted Pyfrom, and my uncles, Sidney and Will, all rode horses. Sidney rode often at Hobby Horse Hall, but my father and Uncle Will were more interested in polo, which was played at Fort Charlotte.

Hobby Horse Hall was the place to be on a Friday afternoon in Nassau. Those were the days when the siren blew at noon from the police station on Bank Lane, and all places of business and all schools closed for the afternoon. The rich and famous among our winter visitors would head west to join throngs of Bahamians for an afternoon of horse racing. Princes and princesses of royal families and of Hollywood could be found among the crowd.

It was sad when the wooden skeleton of the old grandstand came down two years ago. I made a point of taking a picture of it, and as I did, a sense of nostalgia swept over me. A bit of history had truly ended.

All the more reason why Ivan's book is so welcome and so needed!

For too long, too many Bahamians have tended to put our past aside and forget it. We value that which is new and foreign more than those things that are part of us and our past. We see the results of this neglect especially in the loss of so many of our beautiful old buildings.

Our heritage is rich and fascinating, but future generations of Bahamians will never know about it unless there are more enterprising people like Ivan. I commend him for his commitment and dedication. Clearly it has taken many years to complete this research and share with us the information he has uncovered.

It is my hope that Ivan James' work on horse racing in the Bahamas will be well received and widely read by Bahamians of all ages. It is a valuable documentary of a little known, exciting aspect of our past.

Lynn Pyfrom Holowesko, CBE, JP
11 March 2014

He never had a horse, but the sport of kings was his passion, so much so that Ivan James has researched the history of horse racing in the Bahamas from 1782 until its ignominious closure in 1977, leaving starving racehorses to the mercy of the elements. Many of the horses were later flown to Florida by the Broward County Humane Society for adoption.

Mr. James traces Hobby Horse Hall back to the times of Colonel Andrew Deveaux, who drove the Spanish from Fort Nassau and ushered in the Dunmore era.

Lord Dunmore arrived as royal governor in 1787 and quickly selected Barnett Hill, overlooking the harbor's western entrance to build the historic Fort Charlotte to protect the colony from further hostile intrusions. It is recorded that the track was designed and built at the same time as the fort. Mr. James noted that 126 years later, a writer referred to Hobby Horse Hall as the Dunmore Track.

And then the author wickedly asked, "Having an equestrian background, did Governor Dunmore direct his engineering department to design and build Hobby Horse Hall Racecourse out of the King's Treasury for his personal enjoyment?"

The name Hobby Horse Hall seems to have been the original name of the track, which remained with it until the day of its closure. Hobby Horse Hall was included in the 420 acres tract of Crown land granted to Colonel Deveaux.

Its name first appeared on March 31, 1795, when an advertisement for its lease for any term, not less than one nor more than seven years, was published. Said the advertisement:

"The Farm situated four miles west of the town of Nassau known by the name of Hobby Horse Hall, containing 104 acres, forty of which are under good fence. On the premises are a good comfortable dwelling house, and excellent kitchen and a Negro Houser. Apply John Cunningham."

Over the years, horse racing became commercial, moving from the gentry who rode for pleasure to the common folk who turned a good profit at the betting tables.

In the years when Fridays were half days for the town, one could be certain that Hobby Horse Hall was crowded and betting was fierce. Much money was made and lost at "the track" as Bahamians crowded the pari-mutuel windows.

"It is interesting to note," writes Mr. James, "that horse racing became the first national sport of the colony of the Bahamas and the United States of America, where slave jockeys like Austin Curtis, Ned and Monkey Simon, rode their way to freedom in Virginia and North and South Carolina, known as the racehorse region of the United States. In the colony of the Bahamas, only gentlemen riders were allowed."

In 1863, a journalist commenting on the racing frenzy of Bahamians noted that in the colony the leading sports were horse racing, football, rugby, and cricket. "No junkanoo!" commented Mr. James.

Horse racing bills were debated and passed in the House of Assembly. On March 14, 1846, a horse racing bill, Ninth of Victoria, no. 88, chapter 15, was passed. The Queen's Treasury agreed an annual grant of £100 to the Bahamas Turf Club for colonial purse races to be used as an incentive for residents to improve the breed of racehorses.

Over the years, horse racing grew and prospered. It reflected the social history of these islands as more and more Bahamians participated in the sport of kings.

The day in 1977 that Nigel Ingraham, racing secretary and handicapper, called Ivan James from the stands to fill in as the sole judge of the two-furlong pole was the day that Ivan James will never forget. He remained in the post for the remainder of that final racing season.

Although the Racing Commission chairman, Frankie Wilson, acknowledged in 1974 that horse racing was a boost for the economy, by the close of the 1977 race season, the story of Hobby Horse Hall was coming to an end. A month after the PLP won its 1977 election, nine placard-bearing horse owners and trainers picketed on Bay Street, demanding an official government statement on the future of horse racing. They maintained that if there was to be no 1978 race season, the Racing Commission should give the owners money from the benevolent fund to help them keep the animals until the season opened.

Hobby Horse Hall never opened again. By November 1977, stray and starving horses were being flown by caring Americans to the U.S. for adoption.

"Hobby Horse Hall," Mr. James concluded, "did not close for the lack of attendance or the enthusiasm of the racing fans, but for the development of the Cable Beach Hotel Casino complex, and no planning for another racetrack for the future. Through the gates of Hobby Horse Hall passed the most important people in the world."

Not only is Mr. James's horse racing documentary interesting but it is a social commentary of the changing mores over a period of 182 years of the Bahamas and its people.

Eileen Carron
Publisher
The Tribune

Images of the Past

Club House Entrance

Front View of the Club House

Rear View of the Club house

View of the Betting Windows

View of the Club House Grounds

View of the Old Tote Board

View of the paddock and Dan Knowles Buses in the back ground

Panoramic view of the race course from the Club House

Dining Room View

View of the Sumptuous Buffet Table

OFFICIAL PROGRAMME

They're OFF!

at
HOBBY HORSE
HALL

EVERY TUESDAY & FRIDAY

JANUARY THRU APRIL

GATES OPEN 1:00 P.M.
POST TIME
2:00 P. M.

DAILY DOUBLE
1ST AND 2ND RACE
ALSO
QUINELLAS
& EXACTAS

LUNCHEON
and
BAR SERVICE

it's COLOURFUL
it's UNIQUE!

Government Supervised Parimutuel Betting

TUESDAY
March 9th, 1965
Price 3/-

BAHAMAS RACECO, LIMITED

THE MEMBERS OF THE RACING COMMISSION

Mr. Franklyn Wilson, M.P. Chairman
Mr. Otis Brown, Deputy Chairman
Mr. Granville "Smiley" Butler
Mr. Sidney Wilson
Mr. Joseph Sweeting
Mr. Brian Snow, Supervisor of Racing
Mrs. J. Pierre, Exec. Secretary

General Manager
Mr. Mario Parotti

Assistant Manager
Mrs. Sylvia Dahllof

Racing Secretary & Handicapper
Mr. N. Ingraham

Pari Mutuel Manager
Mr. Algie Cartwright

Commission Stewards
Mr. Clifford Rahming

Deputy Stewards
Firnley Palmer

Track Stewards
Mr. P.C. Forsythe
Mr. George Bethell

Hobby Horse Race Track Veterinarian
Dr. Hugh Davis

Racing Commission Veterinarian
Dr. Patrick Balfe

Patrol Judges
Mr. Leonard Miller
Mr. Harold Major
Mr. Leroy Hanna

Placing Judges
Mr. Oswald Cambridge
Mr. Samuel Deveaux
Mr. Henry Williams

Starter
Mr. Abby Lloyd

Paddock Judges
Mr. James Thompson
Mr. L.M. Bowe, Sr.

Jockey Room Master
Mr. Charles Butler

Clerk of Sales
Mr. Richard Russell

Photo Finish
Mr. Hugh Curry

Close Circuit T.V. System
Photo Trackmaster, Inc.

Racing Commission Auditors
Messrs. Sands & Turner

PUBLIC RELATIONS DIRECTORS

"WIN" "PLACE" and "SHOW"

A "WIN" horse is one which finishes First.
A "PLACE" horse is one which finishes First or Second.
A "SHOW" horse is one which finishes First, Second or Third.
In the case of a dead-heat in the Straight Pool, the payoff price shall be figured as in a Place Pool, e.g. holders of Win Tickets on the two horses finishing First will divide the Win Pool, such payoff to be figured as in a Place Pool. Holders of Place Tickets on the aforesaid two horses that dead-heat for first, will divide the Place Pool, such payoff to be figured also as in a regular Place Pool. The next horse will place third and holders of Show Tickets on these three horses will divide the Show Pool.

Analysis

of 15th Meet

The following Horses are entered in the Fifteenth Meet of the Hobby Horse Hall Race Season and represents the Official Clocked Workout Report.

RACING FORM
FIFTEENTH MEET – 22nd FEBRUARY, 1977

AIR KING . . . . Could make Quinella . . . . WT–I.N.A.
AMALONE . . . . . Strong Bet . . . . . . WT-25 1/10 for 2 furlongs, B
BABY TWIST . . . . . Not yet . . . . WT-25 6/10 for 2 furlongs, B
BON BAH ROSE . Should die in sprint. WT-25 3/10 for 2 furlongs, holding
BUNDIO . . . . Outside chance . . . . . . WT-37 9/10 for 3 furlongs, B
BIRD'S EYE . . . . Not yet . . . . WT-26 for 2 furlons, B
CATHERINA . . . . Like her here . . . WT-25 8/10 for 2 furlongs, holding
CONCHA BAY . . . . . . Now or never . . . . . WT-25 1/10 for 2 furlongs, B
COMPLETE IMAGE . Outside chance . WT-25 5/10 for 2 furlongs, holding
CHIME SONG . . Not to be left out . . WT-25 3/10 for 2 furlongs, holding
CAPRICORN Probable key to Quinella .WT-37 1/10 for 3 furlongs, holding
CARMICHAEL QUEEN . . . . Season debut . . . . WT –I.N.A.
CHUTERRO. . . . The one to bet . . . WT-26 2/10 for 2 furlongs, holding
CHINA DOLL . . Looks good here . . WT-25 1/10 for 2 furlongs, holding
CORINA. . . . . Might not be caught . . . WT-38 3/10 for 3 furlongs, B
CIGARILLO. . . . . Contender. . . . . WT–I.N.A.
DOE DOE . . . . . . Should die in sprint . . . WT-25 5/10 for 2 furlongs, B
DAMASCUS. . . . . . Favourite . . . . WT-25 for 2 furlongs, B
DEBI . . . . Not here . . . . 38 4/10 for 3 furlongs, B
DEDI . . . . . . Inside chance . . . . . WT-26 2/10 for 2 furlongs, B
DESPARIDO . . . Should be there. . . WT-25 1/10 for 2 furlongs, holding
DERG . . . . ???. . . . . WT–I.N.A.
E.V.'s CHILD . . Good place to score. . . WT-25 5/10 for 2 furlongs, B
FOREST FIRE 11 . . . . First time out . . . . . . WT–I.N.A.
GONE AWAY . . . . . Inside chance. . . . . .WT-24 6/10 for 2 furlongs, B
FIRST AFFAIR. . . . . Favourite . . . . WT-24 8/10 for 2 furlongs, holding
HOCUS POCUS. . . . . Strong choice . . . . WT–I.N.A.
HOT TOMATO . . . . . Not yet . . . . . WT-25 3/10 for 2 furlongs, B
IDLE DICE . . . . No . . . . . . WT-26 5/10 for 2 furlongs, holding
JUNE'S JOY. . . . . . In hot water. . . . . WT–26 4/10 for 2 furlongs, B
JACKIE . . . . . Not with these . . . . WT-25 4/10 for 2 furlongs, B
JESSICA . . . . Contender . . . . . . WT-26 for 2 furlongs, holding
JUNGLE JOHN. Unimpressive thus far WT26 2/10 for 2 furlongs, holding
KIMBO. . . . . Dropped here . . . . WT–I.N.A.
LUNA 11 . . . . Watch out for her . . . . WT–I.N.A.
LADY ROLLE . . . . First time . . . . WT–I.N.A.
LADY MARINA . . Good spot to score . . WT-25 3/10 for 2 furlongs, B
MELINDA . . . . Don't like her here . . . . WT–I.N.A.
MISS SHARON . . . . . Contender . . . WT-25 1/10 for 2 furlongs, B
MR. JOHN. . . . . No. . . . . . . WT–25 2/10 for 2 furlongs, B
MA CHERI . . . . Inside chance . . . . WT–I.N.A.
MISS GLO. . . . Don't like her here . . . WT-25 1/10 for 2 furlongs, B
MISS H & T . . . . . . No, no, no . . . . . .WT-26 6/10 for 2 furlongs, B
MAMA BRITE . . . . Contender . . . . WT–I.N.A.
MR. BRITE . . . . Favourite . . . . WT–I.N.A.
MIGHTY JOE YOUNG . . . . ??? . . . . WT–I.N.A.
MY ACCOUNT . . . . . . No . . . . WT–25 for 2 furlongs, B
MISS MARSHA BAR. . . . . Don't leave out . . . . WT–I.N.A.
MISS DOREEN . . Look out for this one. . .WT-25 1/10 for 2 furlongs, B
NADO'S CHILD . . In hot water . . WT–25 5/10 for 2 furlongs, holding
PAPA DOPPERLAS . . . . . Contender . . . WT-25 3/10 for 2 furlongs, B
PEPPER WINE . . . Distance against it . . WT-25 1/10 for 2 furlongs, B
PATCH OF WHITE. . . . . Coming. . . . . WT-25 3/10 for 2 furlongs, B
PEACE MAKER . . . . . . Don't like here . . . . . WT-27 for 2 furlongs, F
POETRY IN MOTION . . . . . No . . . . WT-26 4/10 for 2 furlongs, holdin
RED PIGGY BANK . . . No, no, no . . . . Wt-25 2/10 for 2 furlongs, B
REAL NEWS . . . . Don't like it . . . . WT–I.N.

REGAL STAR . . . . Contender . . . . WT–I.N.A
SWEETNESS . . . . ???. . . . . WT–I.N.A.
SUMMER BREEZE. . . . . Inside chance. . . . . WT–I.N.A.
SIR NATIVE . . . . . Not here . . . . . . WT-25 5/10 for 2 furlongs, B
SURENO SPY. . . . .???. . . . . WT–I.N.A.
SECRET AGENT. . . . . . . No . . . . WT-25 for 2 furlongs, B
SOUTHERN FLAME. . Quinella key . WT-24 5/10 for 2 furlongs, holding
STAR OF GEMINI . . . . One to bet. . . . . WT–I.N.A.
STARGAZER . . . .??? . . . . WT–I.N.A.
SOPHIA . . . . . Good choice . . . WT-25 7/10 for 2 furlongs, holding
TORINO . . . . Not here . . . . .WT-25 for 2 furlongs, B
TAMICO . . . . . Not here . . . . . . WT-25 1/10 for 2 furlongs, B
TOP EXECUTIVE . . . . Favourite . . . . WT–I.N.A.
TUDOR MINSTREL . . Favourite . WT-25 4/10 for 2 furlongs, holding
TOP SECRET . . Should get caught . . WT-25 6/10 for 2 furlongs, holding
TAKITA. . . . . . . Strong bet . . . . WT-26 for 2 furlongs, holding
VON HERB . . . . Contender . . . . WT–I.N.A.
WATERGATE. . . . . Favourite . . . . WT–I.N.A.
WAIT FOR ME . . . Not here. . . . . .WT-25 4/10 for 2 furlongs, B
WIND BRINKER . . . . Inside chance . . . . WT–I.N.A.
WINSOME CHARLIE . . . . Threat . . . . WT–I.N.A.

Name of Horses	4F	5F	6F	8F	9F
Arctic Prince					
Appian Way	.53 2/10	1.08	1.33 1/10		
Ant	.54 9/10	1.11 2/10			
Amstel	.53 6/10	1.10 9/10	1.25 2/10	1.50	
Atac	.54		1.23		
Anzac II	.56 2/10				
Anomos			1.25		
Alteza	.54 5/10				
Butterfly II	.53 5/10		1.22 2/10		
Bosman	.56 3/10	1.13			
Beauty			1.30	2.03 8/10	
Buster	.56 9/10			2.06 4/10	
Big Smear				1.55 5/10	
Baby Face					
Bold Venture	.53 9/10	1.09 1/10	1.21 6/10		
Betsy	.56		1.25 6/10		
Black Patch		1.06 4/10	1.31	1.37 5/10	
Beware		1.11 2/10	1.24 7/10		
Bob	.55 3/10	1.09 8/10	1.25	2.00 7/10	
Ball O Fire	.55 1/10	1.07 5/10	1.24 8/10	1.53 8/10	
Baby Doll			1.18		
Bandit	.54	1.08 1/10	1.25 3/10		
Bijou		1.14	1.23 2/10		
Borrasco	.51 9/10	1.06 4/10	1.26 6/10		
Bold Weevil	.52 8/10	1.05 8/10	1.18 3/10	1.53	
Bahama Queen	.57				
Co-CheeNee	.55 2/10	1.09 8/10			
Cola	.53 8/10	1.08			
Cosmo	.54 8/10		1.24	1.58 7/10	
Cosmonette	1.08	1.33 8/10			
Checker King		1.05 8/10	1.20 2/10		
Cinderella			1.26		
Champ		1.08 2/10	1.24 2/10		
Christine		1.12 1/10	1.23		
Chakita		1.07 7/10		1.55 8/10	
Candy	.57 6/10		1.23 3/10		
Contest	.53 2/10		1.22 8/10	1.53 6/10	
Cave Man					
Cupid	.56 6/10				
Cindy (Nikita)	.56 5/10	1.11 5/10			
Coast Guard		1.06	1.28 2/10		
Cavalcade	.56 1/10	1.14 1/10	1.21	2.02 2/10	
Capt. Bill	.56	1.12 1/10			
C-Me-Go			1.27 5/10		
Casanova			1.25 2/10		
Castro	.55				
City Pride					
Cunado					
Case Ace				1.56 1/10	
Conya Bravo	.57 2/10	1.12 7/10	1.20	1.47 5/10	
Canada Dry	.53	1.08	1.29 6/10		
Chippawa	.57 9/10	1.15 6/10			
Donna Alicia	.55	1.09 8/10	1.31		
Dale Star	.54 8/10	1.06	1.21		
Diamond	.54 1/10		1.21 7/10		
Donna					
Encino	.55 2/10				
Early Times	.53 2/10	1.07 5/10			
El Commandante					
El Cid					
Fisherman	.53 1/10				
Forget-Me-Not	.55		1.18 9/10		
Friendships			1.28 1/10		
Child	.51 8/10	1.07 2/10			
Flaming Fire			1.19 9/10	1.51	
Fox Hill	.53 1/10	1.09 9/10		1.56	
Glory	.54 5/10	1.06 6/10	1.26		
Gypsy	.57 7/10	1.11 7/10	1.24 6/10	1.55 7/10	
Gallant Lady		1.08 4/10		1.53 6/10	
Goldstone	.54 3/10	1.08 2/10	1.21 6/10		
Gypsy Prince		1.12 1/10		1.56 1/10	

TICKETS
From
HOBBY HORSE HALL RACE TRACK

1st Half Daily Double CLASS M **4½ fur.**

6-12 YR. OLDS
A HANDICAP RACE

NO QUINELLA BETTING

	WIN	PLACE	SHOW
	2	1	7
			4

1st RACE 1:00p.m.

MAKE SELECTION BY NUMBER

OWNER	TRAINER	Jockey/Morn.Line

1 Oraise Adamson / E. Rolle / J.Sweeting
Red & White Checkers Mts. on Back
BABY TWIST 115

R	F	S	T
4			

9-1

6 yr. (M), Bay, Dam:Tam Twist, Sire: No Seats John

2 Roderick B. Coakley / G. Evans / D.Thompson
Green, White Circle 'G'
CATHERINA 116

R	F	S	T
4	1	1	

4-1

9 yr. (M),Brown, Dam:Olive,Sire: Fleeting Pat

3 Charles E. Moss, Jr. / W. Williams / R.Taylor
Green White Polka Dots
PAPA DOPERLAS 113

R	F	S	T
6	1	1	

3-1

9yr.(G),Roan, Dam:Handy,Sire: Pie Maker

4 Levarity Deveaux / V. Thompson / D.Thompson
Gold Red Circle V On Back
SHASADA 120

R	F	S	T
4			

3-1

8yr.(M) Sorrel, Dam:Modern Art, Sire: Lightning Bug

5 Velthia Rolle / J. Stubbs /
Blue
MELINDA (Tara) 114

R	F	S	T
5	1		

7-1

9yr.(M),Sorrel, Dam:Cindy, Sire: Rango

6 Myrtis Major / J. McKenzie / H.Horton
Blue 3 Gold Bars
CONCHA BAY 118

R	F	S	T
6	3	3	

8-1

11yr.(M),Bay,Dam:Concha Debe,Sire:My Concho King

7 Wilfred Knowles / Adwis Hall /
Red & White
MISS SHARON 119

R	F	S	T
8	3	3	

4-1

8yr. (M),Dun,Dam:Dixie's Delight,Sire:Quick Hanover

8 Ambrose Hanna / D. Lewis / A.Saunders
Black & Gold Heart on Back
SWEETNESS 114

R	F	S	T
2			

5-1

6yr.(M)Grey, Dam:Dandy, Sire:Colorexqun

9 Stephanie Bowe / C. Moxey /
Orange & Black
DOE DOE 118

R	F	S	T

10-1

9yr.(S),Bay,Dam:Blue Skies,Sire:No Seats John

ALSO ELIGIBLES: KIMBO 120; WALLEYE 118; MISS GTO 115;
LADY MARY 120; GOLD GAIL 124

Handicappers Tips: 3, 4, 2, 7

2nd Half Daily Double **2 fur.**

OPEN ENTRY

1st quinella

	WIN	PLACE	SHOW
	9	8	1
			4

2nd RACE 1:40p.m.

MAKE SELECTION BY NUMBER

OWNER	TRAINER	Jockey/Morn.Line

1 Harold Curry / Murray Bain /
Red White Circle
COMPLETE IMAGE 116

R	F	S	T
3	3		

5-1

8yr.(M),Roan,Dam:Satin Blossom,Sire:Little John Olat

2 Garnett Morris / Prince Davis /
Orange & Black
CHIME SONG 120

R	F	S	T
4			

4-1

8yr.(M),Sorrel, Dam:Shula Sire:Spanish Cherse

3 Ronald Kemp / Adwis Hall /
Red & White
TORINO 115

R	F	S	T
5	1	1	

5-1

8yr.(M)Bay,Dam:Little Poco Pep,Sire:Zizzle Sue

4 Kermit Campbell / C. Moxey /
Orange & Black
SUMMER BREEZE 117

R	F	S	T
4	1		

6-1

4 yr.(S)Bay,Dam:Ring Of Fire,Sire:No Seats Jonn

5 Judy Deveaux / V. Thompson /
Gold Red Circle V On Back
JUDE 117

R	F	S	T
4	2		

7-1

4 yr.(M),Bay, Dam: Gem, Sire:Bardoo Boy

6 Linda M. Taylor / J. Stubbs /
Blue
TAMICO 120

R	F	S	T
6	1	1	

5-1

8yr.(M)Sorrel,Dam:Picalites Babs,Sire:Magnitude

7 Tyrone Miller / T. Miller /
Red & White
RED PIGGY BANK 120

R	F	S	T
6			

10-1

11yr.(M),Sorrel,Dam:Lums Baby,Sire:Bank Stosh

8 Clifford Galanis / E. Rolle / J.Sweeting,Jr.
Red & White Checkers Mts. On Back
WATERGATE 120

R	F	S	T
3	2	1	

3-1

4yr.(M)Bay, Dam: Apollo Eleven Sire:Trouble Man

9 Melvin Godet / M. Godet / A.Gibbs
Blue & White Checker
HOCUS POCUS 118

R	F	S	T
13	1	1	

3-1

4 yr.(M),Chestnut, Dam:Baby Boonie,Sire: No Seats John

ALSO ELIGIBLES: MR. JOHN 118

Handicappers Tips: 8, 9, 2, 1

2nd quinella — CLASS M — A HANDICAP RACE — 2-3 YR. OLDS — 6 fu

3rd RACE 2:15 p.m.

WIN 7 PLACE 3 SHOW 4-1

MAKE SELECTION BY NUMBER

OWNER	TRAINER	Jockey/Morn.Line

1 Joseph Grammatico — H. Burrows — B.Richardson
Red Black Diamond — 116
WAIT FOR ME — R F S T / 4 1 1 — 8-1
2yr. (M) Dk. Bay. Dam: Italian Rose; Sire: No Seats John

2 Felix Seymour — E. Rolle — 117
Green White Circle G
AIR KING — R F S T / 4 1 1 — 4-1
3 yr. (B).Bay. Dam: Ali Queen. Sire: Mouie

3 E.V. Walker — T. Demeritte — 117
All Gold Red Circle D in Blue
E.V's. CHILD — R F S T / 3 1 — 3-1
2 yr. (M) Chestnut. Dam: Nato's Child; Sire: Pie Maker(TB)

4 Rowena Sweeting — J. Sweeting — J.Sweeting Jr.
Yellow Green Polka Dots — 114
SIR NATIVE — R F S T / 6 — 7-1
4yr.(B)Chestnut,Dam:Miss Dorone;Sire:No Seats John

5 Anthony Gibson — V. Johnson — C.Patton
White Red Sash — 113
MISS BOLERO — R F S T / 8 1 1 — 8-1
5yr.(M).Red. Dam:Easter Lady,Sire:Bolerolero

6 Philip Kemp — T.E. Demeritte — 115
All Gold Green Polka Dots
PEPPER WINE — R F S T / 4 — 7-1
4yr.(M),Dk.Bay,Dam:Waterlily,Sire:No Seats

7 Vernetta Moss — W. Williams — A.Saunders
Green White Polka Dots — 117
DAMASCUS — R F S T / 2 1 1 — 5-2
2yr.(M) Bay. Dam:Desparino; Sire: Bolerolero (TB)

8 William R. Curtis — E. Rolle — 116
White and White Checkers MT. on Back
MA CHERI — R F S T / 6 1 2 1 — 4-1
4yr.(B),Lt.Bay.Dam:Sherry Sire:No Seats John

9 Matthew Knowles — W. Williams — E.Smith Jr.
Green White Polka Dots — 116
PATCH OF WHITE — R F S T / 2 — 8-1
4yr.(B), Lt.Brown Dam:Demi Price,Sire:Cunado

ALSO ELIGIBLES:

Handicappers Tips: 7, 3, 2, 8

3rd quinella — CLASS K — A HANDICAP RACE — 6 fur

4th RACE 2:45 p.m.

WIN 2 PLACE 8 SHOW 6-7

MAKE SELECTION BY NUMBER

OWNER	TRAINER	Jockey/Morn.Lin

1 Trissie Knowles — Tracy Brown — 118
White Black Spade
SURENO SPY — R F S T / 8 — 8-
4yr.(B)Dark Bay. Dam: Forsythia;Sire:Sanilossa

2 Alphonso Elliott — E. Rolle — 120
Red White Checkers MT on Back
TOP EXECUTIVE (TB) — R F S T — 6-
2yr.(B) Bay. Dam: Alan Bebel(TB); Sire:Good Behavine(TB)

3 Thomas Ferguson — H. Burrows — S.Hamilton
Red & Gold Diamond — 116
MISS H & T (Step In Line) — R F S T / R 1 — 10-
8yr.(M),Sorrel.Dam:Junee Cindy;Sire:Fort Osage

4 Jacklyn Carroll — E. Williams — E.Smith.Jr.
Black Red Circle C On Back — 112
DEBI — R F S T / 6 — 5-
10 yr.(M).Bay. Dam:Anna Beri Barton;Sire:Sir Hewley

5 Denzil Rolle — J. Stubbs — 113
Yellow & Red Shirt
IDLE DICE (No Seats Jane) — R F S T / 6 — 6-
6 yr.(M). Dam: Rowdy Jand,Sire: No Seat Jane

6 Arlene Chipman — B. Musgrove — B.Arthur
Red & Gold — 119
REAL NEWS — R F S T / 8 2 3 1 — 6-
3yr.(M)Bay.Dam:Heavy Heddy,Sire:Just Right

7 Enid Lewis — D. Lewis — 119
Black With Gold Cross
DEDI — R F S T / 5 — 4-
8yr.(M),Chestnut.Dam: Redwing Trinket,Sire:Musho Rex

8 Pauline Williams — L. Wallace — H.Cartwright
White with Red Circle on Back — 117
MISS GLO — R F S T / 8 2 1 — 4-
10yr.(M),Dun,Dam:Irish Angel;Sire:Roman Crown

9 Patrick W. Bethel — T.E. Demeritte — A.Saunders
All Gold Circle D in Blue — 116
TUDOR MINSTREL — R F S T / 2 1 — 5-
4yr.(B)Bay. Dam:Tudor Miss;Sire:No Seats John

ALSO ELIGIBLES: ITALIAN ROSE 118; BOLD CHILD 118

Handicappers Tips: 2, 9, 7, 8

SIXTH RACE
Approx. 5:20
FOUR FURLONGS

Quinella

MAKE SELECTION BY NUMBER

POST POSITION		
1	Hortense Bowe — J. Marshall Black and White **CAVALCADE**	**106**
2	Myrtle Dorsett — G. Greenslade Green and White **SQUARE MEASURE**	**110**
3	T. L. Hilton — J. Godet White, Blue Sash **SIR GREG**	**104**
4	Ellen Burrows — A. H. Knowles Red, Black Diamond **RED ROSE**	**106**
5	Ulric Holgerson — E. S. McGregor Yellow, Blue and Red **SHORT NAIL**	**104**
6	Louise Griffeth — T. Demeritte Gold, Blue Circle with D in Red **MEDICINE**	**116**
7	Gloria Major — G. Evans Blue and Gold **GOLDSTONE**	**111**
8	Ethel Bowe — E. S. McGregor Blue and Purple **JIMMY JR.**	**107**
9	Tex Lunn — H. Strachan Orange and Black **FOX HILL**	**110**
10		

SUBSTITUTES

TRACK SELECTIONS
6—7—9

Horse Stables No. 1 Barn

Inside of the Stables

Horse Stables No. 2 Barn

Racing Steward's Tower

Photo-finish Tower of the Judges

Front view of the old Club House

The Bahamas First Sporting Seat
Eighteen Decades of Racing
1792-1977

The first documented one mile Oval Race Course in the
Western World where ordinary lives become
extraordinary!

Index